Humanitarian Intervention

1- 11 -33 -35

Point/Counterpoint

Philosophers Debate Contemporary Issues
General Editors: James P. Sterba and Rosemarie Tong

This new series will provide a philosophical angle to debates currently raging in academic and larger circles. Each book will be a short volume (around 200 pages) in which two prominent philosophers debate different sides of an issue. Future topics might include the canon, the ethics of abortion rights, and the death penalty. For more information contact Professor Sterba, Department of Philosophy, University of Notre Dame, Notre Dame, IN 46566, or Professor Tong, Department of Philosophy, Davidson College, Davidson, NC 28036.

Political Correctness: For and Against
    Marilyn Friedman, Washington University, St. Louis
    Jan Narveson, University of Waterloo, Ontario, Canada

Humanitarian Intervention: Just War vs. Pacifism
    Robert L. Phillips, University of Connecticut
    Duane L. Cady, Hamline University

Humanitarian Intervention

Just War vs. Pacifism

by
Robert L. Phillips and Duane L. Cady

Rowman & Littlefield Publishers, Inc.

ROWMAN & LITTLEFIELD PUBLISHERS, INC.

Published in the United States of America
by Rowman & Littlefield Publishers, Inc.
4720 Boston Way, Lanham, Maryland 20706

3 Henrietta Street
London WC2E 8LU, England

British Cataloging in Publication Information Available

Library of Congress Cataloging-in-Publication Data

Phillips, Robert L. (Robert Lester), 1938–
Humanitarian intervention : just war vs. pacifism / by Robert L. Phillips and
Duane L. Cady.
p. cm. — (Point/counterpoint)
Includes bibliographical references and index.
1. Intervention (International law) I. Cady, Duane L. II. Title. III. Series.
JX4481.P43 1996 341.5'84—dc20 95–42477 CIP

ISBN 0–8476–8141-6 (cloth : alk. paper)
ISBN 0–8476–8142-4 (pbk. : alk. paper)

Printed in the United States of America

♾™ The paper used in this publication meets the minimum requirements of
American National Standard for Information Sciences—Permanence of
Paper for Printed Library Materials, ANSI Z39.48–1984.

Contents

Preface

Humanitarian intervention is an increasingly complex and difficult subject. Instant communication, rapid international transportation, an increasingly global economy, advancing technologies, and weapons proliferation all have complicated and intensified political turmoil in our post-cold war world. When combined with hosts of unresolved historical animosities, contemporary conditions affecting possibilities for an orderly and sustained peaceful community of nations nearly overwhelm anyone attempting to think through the relevant moral issues.

In what follows, we reflect on humanitarian intervention as philosophers. Our efforts are attempts to clarify important relevant concepts and to examine relevant principles, assumptions, and values. We approach this consideration of humanitarian intervention from very different perspectives: the just war tradition and the pacifist tradition. We begin with very different values and we come to very different conclusions, yet readers will note that along the way we find connections between these seemingly polar opposites, and we discover some common ground.

The scope of our discussion includes a variety of cases, many of which appear daily in the various news media. We do not pretend to exhaust the range of cases relevant to our topic, nor do we attempt comprehensive consideration of the cases we discuss. Rather, familiar cases are used to exemplify problems and issues, to illustrate points we wish to make, or to explore implications of the value positions in question.

Since we begin—and end—this collaborative work with very different positions, the project takes the form of a debate. Each of us offers a lead essay articulating our perspective on humanitarian intervention. These were written independently, without our having discussed substantive differences in our views. With the response essays we each attempt to answer the other's lead essay. We did not negotiate over what was or was not a fair and reasonable interpretation of our work nor did we attempt to alter one another's response. We leave such tasks to the reader.

We wish to thank Jim Sterba, the Point/Counterpoint series editor, for inviting us—and convincing us—to participate in this exchange. It has been a challenging and engaging experience that we hope contributes to ongoing conversations about these difficult issues. We are grateful also to Jennifer Ruark, acquisitions editor, and Julie Kuzneski, production editor, for their help in seeing this project through to completion. Finally, thanks go to our institutions for their support and especially to our families for their love and encouragement.

The Ethics of Humanitarian Intervention

The Problem of Intervention

The problem of the intervention of one state in the affairs of another is not new but has taken on a greater urgency and sharper focus in the decade following the demise of the Soviet Union. The fifty years of the cold war, although materially and spiritually debilitating, imposed an international order wherein military interventions were somewhat structured and restrained. This happened in two ways; first, no interventions, whatever the pretext, could be entirely divorced from the ideological and geopolitical balance of power. Indeed, it may be said that interventions were aimed primarily at preserving that balance. From the geopolitical perspective, the task of the United States and its allies during the long period of confrontation was to prevent the Soviet Union and its allies from consolidating power on the Eurasian land mass, that great "world island" that contains most of the world's population, resources, and geopolitical perspective. In this sense, the United States merely continued the policy carried out by the British over the preceding five hundred years. Hence, there is a sense in which all the interstate wars of modern European history are the same war. As with Bonaparte, the Kaiser, and Hitler, the cold war sought to prevent Eurasian hegemony on the part of any single power or alliance of powers. For not only would such an outcome be inherently dangerous, but also the hegemonic power, having consolidated its position, would be poised for global power projection.

The ideological dimension of the cold war also conditioned interventions. Marxism, as filtered through Russian history, was

1

incompatible with the Judeo-Christian conception of man. In fact, it was a system built on deliberate falsification of reality. As such, it eventually suffocated in its own lies. In the meantime, Marxism was able to mobilize many people around the globe, not the least of which were intellectuals in the West, especially in the universities. Questions of intervention thus always had a sharp ideological dimension, most clearly in the case of the Vietnam War.

The second sense in which military interventions were structured and restrained during the cold war was the omnipresence of the nuclear threat. Extreme caution had to be exercised regarding any intervention, regardless of its scope and geographical location. There was simply no way of knowing whether any intervention would start the powder train to nuclear holocaust. It was over a projected U.S. intervention in Cuba that the world came as close as it ever has to nuclear war. A distinguishing feature of the cold war period was that the strategy adopted by the west to deal with Soviet hegemonic aspirations tended to maximize temptations to intervention, temptations that were simultaneously dampened by fears of nuclear war. The strategy of containment proposed by George Kennan in 1947 was adopted by the United States in its essentials. Containment envisioned encircling the Soviet Union with economic and military alliances until such time as communism collapsed under the weight of its internal contradictions. While this is in fact what happened, critics at the time pointed out that containment would force the West to ally itself with an array of morally unsavory client states and to prop them up, often against the wishes of their citizens. Moreover, as containment is a balance-of-power strategy, the Soviets would be constantly testing the balance, thus requiring the United States to intervene continually around the Soviet perimeter. Indeed, the Soviets made frequent attempts to push through cold war boundaries (in Korea, Vietnam, and Berlin) or to leapfrog containment (in Cuba, Nicaragua, and Angola). There is a certain irony in all this. Balance of power in the guise of containment was frequently defended as a morally superior alternative to World War III, yet balance of power invites a multiplicity of conflicts as each side probes the weak points of the other.

Overall, containment was a success because Soviet strategy was, in any case, hegemony by attrition, not by overt warfare. In general, it may be said that interventions throughout the cold war were often counterproductive. Many small third-world nations became, however willingly, cold war pawns whose development was stifled or set back by the game of geopolitics. Ethiopia, Somalia, and Angola are obvious cases, as are Cuba and Nicaragua, but there are many others. The major powers did not escape either. Vietnam and Afghanistan turned sour when the would-be beneficiaries of intervention proved ungrateful or uncomprehending. As we shall discover, there is often a very large gap between the (sometimes) good intentions of the interveners and the carrying out of an operation. There are many reasons for this, the primary one being that an army is an extremely blunt instrument for carrying out an act of charity and many good intentions become lost in the fog of war. We must be clear at the outset that there are no "surgical strikes" and that "limited objectives" rarely are. An analysis of interventions must keep clearly focused not only on intentions (where most of the public debate seems to be) but also on means and likely outcome.

The cold war generated an interesting shift in perceptions about the purpose of military establishments. Modern armies and their traditions and practices are descended from European and classical Greek class notions (officers and men) about violence as ennobling and morally regenerative. While World War I put a large dent in this view, it took the cold war to alter public perspectives. Much has been written about the "Vietnam syndrome" as if it were an isolated virus from which America should try to recover as quickly as possible. But Vietnam may well have been merely an illustration of a large-scale trend away from the efficacy of war in the modern world. Whatever the truth of that perception, public opinion, as well as military doctrine in the industrial countries, continued to shift during the cold war in favor of a strategy wherein deterrence was seen as the prime function of the military. As noted, this was in part due to the nuclear Sword of Damocles but also to an awareness that the cost and destructiveness of modern *conventional* weaponry had begun to exceed the benefits. The secretary of defense during the Reagan years, Caspar Weinberger, was brought to formulate a set of criteria for the activation of U.S. forces of such stringency that it was widely joked to have brought about the end of warfare. Hence, as we entered the post-cold war era, public opinion as well as that of influential sectors of the military indicated less than full enthusiasm for the use of the military. Moreover, as communism fell through the "velvet revolution" (i.e., nonviolently), there was even deeper uncertainty over the role of military forces.

The Bush administration began with a search for an international system to replace the order imposed by the strategy of containment. The much-vaunted "New World Order" accompanied by "end of history" theme music very quickly got nowhere. In considering the ethics of intervention, it is very important to examine why this is so. In doing so, we see that the past fifty years form a pattern of successively failed attempts to create a supranational system to deal with the perceived problem of international anarchy. This view, which has more or less dominated, may be traced back to the Enlightenment insistence on the primacy and universality of Reason. In a famous incident of the French Revolution, a party of revolutionaries entered the cathedral of Notre Dame and replaced the crucifix from the high altar with a statue of a beautiful young woman, the goddess of Reason. Thus, a religion of spirituality was replaced with a rationalist ideology that was antithetical to the historical particularity of the Incarnation. This Enlightenment committed to universal Reason carried with it a corresponding antipathy to the particularity of peoples, nations, ethnicity, and religion. But successive efforts to transcend nationalism, culminating in a failed Marxist internationalism, suggest something irreducible about national, linguistic, ethnic, and religious groupings. Successive empires, hegemonies, and "new world orders" have come and gone but national groupings remain stronger than ever. There is certainly some truth in the "global village" idea fostered, it seems, mainly by international capitalist enterprises. The ubiquity of certain kinds of movies and clothing should not be taken too seriously, however. Beneath this faddish skin lies the meat of nationalism.

There is no contesting that many forms of intervention have been and continue to be generated by Enlightenment Reason bent on eradicating the "irrationality of particularity," and this goes for at least some cases of humanitarian intervention. Perhaps the clearest recent statement of the irreducible character of cultures is in Pope John Paul II's *Centesimus Annus*. After noting that the fall of Soviet Marxism was partly a result of failed economic theory and practice, John Paul adds that Marxist internationalism and class theory were also factors.

> It is not possible to understand man on the basis of economics alone, nor to define him on the basis of class membership. Man is understood in a more complete way when he is situated within the sphere of culture through his language, history, and the position he takes toward the fundamental events of life, such as birth, work, love, and death. At the heart of every culture lies the attitude man takes to the greatest mys-

tery: The mystery of God. Different cultures are basically different ways of facing the question of the meaning of personal existence. When this question is eliminated, the culture and moral life of nations is corrupted. For this reason the struggle to defend work (in Poland) was spontaneously linked to the struggle for culture and national rights.[1]

This is a profound reflection suggesting that culture (including national culture) forms a basic natural element in human society, much like the family. It is through culture that a human completeness is achieved that is not possible elsewhere. The kind of internationalism so prevalent in many guises in this century is an abstraction, a product, of rationalism. It is only in the cultural context that man finds a complete array of fundamental questions that, as John Paul puts it, bear on the issues of life and death. The connection (or interconnections) among language, culture, and historical experience are reflective of the many dimensions of man. This implies a certain *inviolability* of culture. As a form of human association that has gradually evolved, creating a form of life, there is an organic integrity that may not be readily intruded upon. The moral question of intervention must, therefore, take this kind of fundamental particularity as a datum not subsumed into some higher form. This is another way of stating the principle of subsidiarity, which is a principle of self-help wherein decisions are made at the lowest possible level of administration. The purpose of an intervention must ultimately be to help people to help themselves.

The precise role of community in realizing human good will be explored shortly, but here we can say that particular human associations are not optional but, rather, are the natural matrix for facing the critical value questions of human life. There is, therefore, a strong presumption against any intervention that inhibits this process.

Moral Foundations

While it is true that to tamper with culture is to disturb something intrinsic to the person, it is also true that there is something universal about man. All must be treated justly because all share in a common human nature ordained to a set of specific goods. It is the violation of this universal order by some particularity that raises the issue of intervention. For it is not an adequate answer to the question of intervention to tout the integrity of culture as if that were an absolute. As St. Augustine well put it in *The City of God*, "In the absence of justice, what is sovereignty but organized brigandage? For what are bands of brigands but petty kingdoms?" [2]

It is necessary to sketch out at least briefly the theory of human good. What distinguishes man from all other creatures on earth is his freedom for self-determination. All other creatures fulfill their nature merely in terms of their intrinsic capacities for development. Only man may choose to live according to his nature or in opposition to it. In this way, each choice creates the chooser in one direction or another. The individual is, in effect, a work of art that is never finished until natural death. We are not absolutely free, as God is. Circumstances and natural inheritance condition freedom. But as the marvelous variegation of human history shows, man shapes his future in the face of an openness unknown to the animal kingdom. The question thus becomes: What are the proper objects of our choices? Another way of putting this question is to ask whether there are any prior constraints on human freedom. Many philosophers have, of course, argued that there are no such constraints. Jean Paul Sartre claimed that if we are not created by God, then man is identical with his freedom. Although Sartre goes on (inconsistently) to invoke the notion of responsibility, it is clear that if we are not creatures, if we are not *for* anything, then quite literally, anything goes. Most people would balk at such a conclusion in practice, although it is very easy to get modern people to assent to the theory. The current fad for deconstruction is the latest incarnation of the view that we are identical with our freedom. But when we find a philosophical theory that is incompatible with the way we live, then there is something wrong with the theory. In fact, we clearly know that some choices are better than others. For example, a life devoted to the pursuit of knowledge is better than one mired in ignorance and superstition. This life is better not only in some consequentialist sense but because such a choice for truth makes the chooser better off as such. Similarly, a concern to will the good for another person for that person's sake is a better act than to reduce that person to a use relationship. Genuine human fulfillment is thus predicated on an objective order of human goods. We simply do not always know what is good for us, which would be the case if we were identical with our freedom. People make mistakes in their life choices, but such errors are only possible if there truly are human goods about which one can be mistaken.

Reason can help us to identify these goods. Because such goods are fundamental, the object of our choices, they must be simple and self-evident. Because human freedom is open-ended, the goods, the proper objects of human freedom, must also be open-ended. Examples of such basic human goods are life, knowledge, and friendship. To pursue knowledge is not to seek a specific goal whose acquisition might be fully accomplished but to participate in an ongoing activity that is worth doing for its own sake. Similarly, friendship is not an accomplishment but is ever developing as the friends continually explore new facts of their relationship. It is the participation in such objective human goods that constitutes human fulfillment. Happiness is, thus, accomplished not by having experiences or by having things, but by living well, where living well means maximizing one's opportunities to participate in the basic human goods.

It follows that genuine or integrated human fulfillment requires that we respect the integrity of each basic human good. Human choices must be made in the light of all the goods as these goods are essentially incommensurable. It makes no sense, for example, to try to "weigh" one life against another or to try to balance friendship against knowledge in order to achieve some sort of maximization of good. Because they are open-ended, the goods are not quantifiable. There can be no consequentialist calculus. On this view, evil is the pursuit of one good by means of the suppression of another. A woman seeking an abortion seeks a good for herself of greater life prospects at the expense of the life of the unborn. Two students cheat on an exam to cement their friendship, but they do so at the expense of truth. Human fulfillment can never be achieved in this manner because, quite apart from harming others, such persons cut themselves off from those goods, the participation in which is fulfilling to them. While it is common today to express skepticism regarding an objective moral order, it is not really possible without contradiction to deny such an order while living in the real world. Do skeptics really think that friendship might *not* be a good? Or if someone were to deny that the pursuit of knowledge was a good, what would they be saying? Presumably, their reason for telling us this is because they think it important that we *know* this. So the denial that knowledge is a good is itself a significant piece of knowledge, which it is, presumably, good for us to know. Indeed, to *speak* at all implies a range of human goods, including truth and community.

Further reflection on human goods leads to the conclusion that they cannot be fully realized outside community. This obviously goes for knowledge, which is a cooperative enterprise, and for friendship. But the same is true of life (which requires protection and sustenance), aesthetics, integrity, and religion (which requires, minimally, a relation to God). If the good of others is truly tied up with my good and if human goods have a transcultural character, then the political or cultural boundaries within which I dwell may not be regarded as absolutes. In other words, my obligation to help others in their need is not unconnected with my own fulfillment. The virtue of charity is, thus, central to the moral life because only through self-giving love (which entails a forgetfulness of self) is the self fulfilled. This uncalculated giving is obviously not confined *a priori* to any particular group or political configuration but is potentially directed to all.

Now, it must be admitted that charity as the focus of the moral life is somewhat mysterious: an uncalculating self-giving that is the fulfillment of the self. Yet, anyone who has ever been in love knows experientially the truth of this mystery. A lover cares for nothing but the good of the beloved, is totally absorbed in the other, wishes only to be with the beloved. If asked later when was he the most happy, he will, of course, say, "When I was in love!" We should cleave to lovers rather than to philosophical skeptics. We may seem to be very far from our topic. We are not. The issue of intervention is the question of the range of charity, and if the universality of human goods is a fact, then the range of charity is coextensive with the human community. As with all loves, there is a delicacy of calculation (or perhaps better, insight) regarding this matter. As charity involves intimacy, we must be very cautious not to intrude where we are not wanted. Thus, intervention requires a maturity of judgment, an ability to maintain the essential dignity of the other while providing a self-effacing help. We will find no mechanistic criteria here but only prudence on a foundation of virtue. There is no political science, only a fixed awareness of the good and the will to seek it.

An intervention is a political act, the province of organized national states in the modern world; we must inquire into the purpose of statecraft. It is common since Machiavelli to distinguish between an idealistic and realistic conception of the purpose of the state. A transitional figure, Machiavelli argued that while the Prince should be good when and as he was able to do so (for, after all, it is good to be good), yet he must always be prepared to do evil when necessary. What necessity is this? His answer is the gateway to modernity. The newly emerging national state, Machiavelli believes, provides the sole realm of order. The spiritual order of Christianity has failed to materialize because it is rooted in the idea of justice rather than power. The saint monarch or the Platonic philosopher king is a fiction. Hence, realism demands a political philosophy based upon the absolute sovereignty of the state as the only unit capable of preserving human life. But Machiavelli surely exaggerates the degree of necessary animosity among peoples (as does Hobbes, even more so). No state is really sovereign but is a member of the community of nations. Trade and other commerce are just as much necessities as territorial antagonism. Religion also forms a bridge among nations, even though Machiavelli downgrades this tie. In short, a *Realpolitik* that posits an irreducible antagonism (a permanent war of all against all) is itself unrealistic. No one really wants to live in that kind of world as, among other things, such a world would be extremely dangerous. We are made to live in concord and men naturally seek peace. So we must avoid positing a chasm between morality and realism. Policies that seek to effect peaceful relations among nations *are* the pursuit of realism.

On a more balanced view, the purpose of the state is much what St. Augustine thought it to be: the preservation of a just order among men. If there are basic human goods and if participation in these is the condition of human fulfillment, then the role of the state is to foster these goods and the opportunities for such participation. As community is not an optional choice, we need to recognize that we are members of a larger world community whose good is intimately linked to our own good. No matter how imperfectly such a world is realized in history, there is no choice but to direct the state toward this ideal. To see the state as a form of charity is at once to understand it in an activist sense. The state has duties of commutative and distributive justice not only to its members but to all who form the human community. The *capacity* of the state to undertake this task will depend upon its vitality and that will depend upon a reasonable self-regard. As with any community, leadership will have an obligation first to its members' well-being. A father, for example, has special obligations to care for his children, which he does not have for children in general. But having duly recognized this, his relation to others outside his family does not consist merely of negative duties (e.g., to refrain from harm). He will also have the positive duties of fostering the good of others. Why is this so? Because the basic human goods are open-ended and, therefore, not the possession of anyone. They are common goods that are the condition of human flourishing. Hence, if life or integrity are goods for me, they are also goods for others. Moreover, in the exercise of charity toward those who are suffering lies my own fulfillment, not in some sense of "enlightened self-interest," but in the sense that the fulfillment of self can only come through the forgetfulness of self. As free and self-determining beings we are, by nature, self-transcendent and it is through acts of charity that such transcendence occurs.

This much natural reason can tell us. These deliverances are also derived from, and powerfully reinforced by, Christianity with its roots in Judaism. Hence, it is not a matter of chance that conceptions of human rights, human equality, and democracy developed in the Christian world. It was also this world that generated the idea of international law, international mediating institutions, and tradition of the just use of force. The reasons for this are fairly clear: For Christianity, all men are creations of the same Father and spring from the same primordial parents. Human fate is thus tied to this intimacy of communion. There are no foreigners. Not only are all brothers, but the Incarnational principle enormously enhances human dignity. The fact that God entered history in human form, not *disguised* as a man, but as "true man" divinizes humanity and makes possible the conception of each human being as having infinite dignity and worth. When these revelations are coupled with the idea of God as charity (not the one who loves, but the one who *is* love), whose very being is a dynamic of love, the application to a neighbor is obvious: This is my commandment: Love one another as I have loved you.

This conjunction of reason and revelation forms the basis of Western civilization and, because the world is now largely Westernized, increasingly, of global civilization. While respecting the specific forms that human communities take in history, and while recognizing the truth of Baltasahar's remark, "Truth is symphonic," there is a clear imperative to create a world community of independent self-determining peoples. Given the commonality of human nature, such self-determination may not be directed to merely any end, but to the fostering of basic human goods. That is, the purpose of self-determination is the all-round flourishing of the members of the community. This cannot take place without justice—the rendering to each man his due. Natural justice is properly enforced by the *polis*, but as there is no global *polis*, enforcement of natural justice is the province of civilized states. That this should be done through the machinery of existing international bodies is obviously desirable as one of the key impediments to just intervention is the charge that states intervene only to further some interest of their own. Just as an individual is not a proper judge in his own case, so a nation is not either.

✕ The Problem of Sovereignty

Just interventions involve the use of force and this is, in the end, what makes them problematical. St. Augustine reminded us that the use of force by one person to subjugate another is a consequence of man's fallen nature. We naturally are made for concord and equality as children of the same Father, but due to the disordered passions, we tend to concupiscence, a disordered love of creatures, especially ourselves. Augustine's point is that while the use of force to achieve justice may be necessary as a means to achieve earthly justice, those who are wielding the instruments of force are as weakened in their natures as are the objects of their attack. And he goes on to point out how frequently in human history do the just slide into the unjust. This is a most important warning. Any kind of domination of one by another is a substitute or a shadow of Divine justice; therefore, those undertaking to effect justice by force should do so in a spirit of service to others animated by a lively sense of humility (there but for the grace of God . . .).

It also follows that the use of force must not be entered upon without a deep moral seriousness evinced by a willingness to ask a series of defining questions. These defining questions are known as the tradition of the Just War. As indicated, they consist of a series of questions that any moral person must ask himself before resorting to force.

The set of conditions styled *jus ad bellum* covers questions pertaining to initiating combats. Of specific importance is the "last resort" clause. Especially in the context of intervention where sovereignty is being breached, it is very important that serious efforts be made (and be seen to be made) to find peaceful solutions to the problem. *Jus ad bellum* was devised to deal with the issue of inter-state conflict, the aggression of one state against another. At least

this is how the tradition has developed in the modern era, especially as its provisions have been translated into international law.
However, it is most interesting to note that in the earliest medieval
formulations of theory, *jus ad bellum* specified the obligation of
"Christian princes" to correct injustices that had gone uncorrected
in the realms of other princes. This vigorous sense of the primacy
of natural justice over sovereignty was gradually replaced in the
era of the modern bureaucratic state by conceptions of "absolute"
sovereignty. By the nineteenth century, doctrines of "reasons of
state," whereby national leaders could claim immunity even from
international law (not to mention morality), had come to the fore.
This development was an evolution of the Machiavellian theme that
". . . in the actions of men, and especially of princes, from which
there is no appeal, the end justifies the means." Machiavelli thus
introduced us to a schizophrenic conception of ethics—personal
morality is divorced from statecraft. Privately, a man should pursue
the basic human goods, but the Prince is, perforce, required to shift
into a consequentialist mode in order to "save the state": "Therefore it is necessary for a prince who wishes to maintain himself, to
learn how not to be good, and to use this knowledge and not use it,
according to the necessity of the case." [3]

Hence is born the idea of state necessity. Machiavelli is clear
that in a world of absolute sovereignty, the only hope for the "good
life" is within the context of some *polis*, hence the overriding necessity of preserving the political order at all costs, including moral costs. The Machiavellian model represents a violent rupture of
the natural law tradition and sets the course of Western political
thinking inexorably toward "reasons of state." But, as argued in this
essay, *absolute* sovereignty is a moral fiction. If something is a basic
human good, it is good for all men. In this sense, the human community is paramount not as an administrative unit, but as a moral
order. Within the human community, specific natural forms emerge:
the family, religion, the *polis*. And while these exert special obligations, they do so against the background of a shared human nature.

The intolerable character of absolute sovereignty as a theory,
reaching its zenith in the nineteenth century, was counteracted in
two ways. First, development of the international law and conventions regulating war continued the tradition of Hugo Grotius and
other seventeenth century jurists. In the present century, these efforts issued in the Hague and Geneva Conventions as well as the
League of Nations and the United Nations. Second, and in some

sense underlying the first development, was the theory of national self-determination. On this view, "peoples" have a right to determine the shape of their association, including political association. There is an important grain of truth in this view. As argued above, familial, religious, cultural, and national configurations are critical modes of human relations wherein persons confront the choices that shape them. There has been much discussion of the principle of self-determination and, indeed, there are many objections to it, not the least of which regards the difficulty of precisely specifying what group is to count as "a people." But the key difficulty resides in the fact that the principle of self-determination, as it has evolved, is a reaction to absolute sovereignty and, as such, shares the same absolutist tendencies. It is now frequently proclaimed that every ethnic group has a "right" to its own state. Such claims are preposterous given the manner of distribution of such groups and their sizes. But the problem is not with such groups themselves—they merely take advantage of the quasi-religious status accorded to the principle in many quarters. Rather, the principle is itself fatally vague, failing to specify a workable definition of a "people" or what size a self-determining population has to be. Moreover, why such groups have an overriding right to sovereignty is not argued. Interventions on behalf of such groups are, therefore, morally problematic. Perhaps the requirements for third-party intervention could be significantly lessened if self-determination were not conceived as an all-or-nothing proposition. That is, we might instead adopt a strategy of *protecting* minority groups and their integrity within the larger sovereignty in which they find themselves.

The Challenge of Humanitarian Intervention

In this regard, the most extensive theory of just intervention is that of Michael Walzer in *Just and Unjust Wars*. Walzer accepts the modern order of sovereignty not only as an historical fact but as a moral good. Working from a rights-based theory, he argues that people must not only be understood to have rights, but they must have a place or "space" within which to exercise such rights. Hence, the moral significance of sovereignty is that it provides a protected place for self-determination and for the exercise of human rights. So Walzer (correctly) understands that sovereignty is an instrumental good, not an end in itself, but one that (all things being equal) deserves the very strongest *presumption* of inviolability. Without that presumption by the community of nations, the stability required for long-term choices would be absent. Yet, there may surely be cases where breach of such sovereignty is morally required. In such cases, the burden of proof will fall squarely upon the intervener.

> Sovereignty is the only way we have of establishing an arena within which freedom can be fought for and (sometimes) won. It is this arena and the activities which go on within it that we want to protect, and we protect them, much as we protect individual integrity, by marking out boundaries that cannot be crossed, rights that cannot be violated. As with individuals, so with sovereign states: there are things that we cannot do to them even for their own ostensible good.[4]

Yet Walzer urges that the traditional legal barrier to intervention cannot (from the moral point of view) be absolute, partly because boundaries are not fixed by nature and partly because political communities are not always perfectly homogeneous. Even so, one undertakes an intervention with trepidation. First, because there will always be a suspicion regarding the motives of the intervener. Is the intervention self-serving? Does it matter if it is partly self-serving? Is there self-deception or just plain deception? Second, communities, like individuals, can only flourish if they are free to make self-determining choices. Hence, there is the strongest possible presumption in favor of communal autonomy.

Walzer distinguishes three cases of just intervention: "1. Cases of the breakup of a sovereign state caused by the secession of one faction from the rest. 2. Cases where a country has already been invaded and third parties face the question of counter-intervention. 3. When the violation of human rights within a set of boundaries is so terrible when it makes talk of community or self-determination or arduous struggle seem cynical and irrelevant, that is, in cases of enslavement or massacre." [5]

It is the third sort of intervention that has come to the fore as humanitarian intervention with which we are chiefly concerned. In developing his view, Walzer draws on the argument of J. S. Mill that the internal freedom of a political community can be won only by the members of that community. This view rules out the substitution of foreign intervention for the internal struggle.

> A state is self-determining even if its citizens struggle and fail to establish free institutions, but it has been deprived of self-determination

if such institutions are established by an intrusive neighbor. The members of a political community must seek their own freedom, just as the individual must cultivate his own virtue. They cannot be set free, as he cannot be made virtuous, by any external force. Indeed, political freedom depends upon the existence of individual virtue, and this the armies of another state are most unlikely to produce . . . self-determination is the school in which virtue is learned (or not) and liberty is won (or not).[6]

There is, Walzer claims, a specific sort of exception to this general rule, which he (correctly) regards as, in general, a good one. The imperative to self-help presupposes a level of political peace that renders long-term choices possible, where people are under such massive oppression as to make the very idea of self-determination nonsensical. "When a people are being massacred, we don't require that they pass the test of self-help before coming to their aid. It is their very incapacity which brings us in." [7]

Consequently, humanitarian intervention is less like conventional military intervention and more like domestic police work. Walzer seems to be saying that when a state so oppresses its people to the point that they are unable to resist, such a state gives up clear title to sovereignty. And while legally the title remains in international law, morally there is a duty of charity to intervene. "People who initiate massacres lose their right to participate in the normal (even in the normally violent) process of domestic self-determination. Their military defeat is morally necessary."[8]

Walzer's arguments for humanitarian intervention were first stated in 1977. In the context of the cold war and of the state of international law, he necessarily sharply contrasted the legal situation (the legalist paradigm) with the requirements of ethics. But with the fall of the Iron Curtain and the subsequent New World Disorder, the system of international law has rapidly begun to reflect the moral arguments advanced by Walzer and, of course, those earlier defenders of natural justice.

Turning again to the post-cold war situation, we find a remarkable change of attitude as well as of policy. As noted above, *jus gentium* had evolved into a rigid doctrine of absolute sovereignty by the end of the nineteenth century. This meant that states were strictly prohibited from interfering in the affairs of other states. "Internal" affairs were understood to include such diverse matters as the form of government, the structure of the constitution with its due apportionment of rights and duties, the economic system (and, thereby, the definition and implementation of distributive justice), and the social relations among members of the community. In short, sovereignty was construed to cover all relations between citizens and government and among citizens as specified by law or custom.

The conceptual and historical evolution of this position, radical though it is, is not difficult to follow. Under the traditional theory of statecraft, of which *bellum justum* was a department, it was axiomatic that a Christian prince was duty bound to correct injustices in the realm of delinquent rulers. Such was the duty of charity that knew no bounds. This view began to deteriorate with the Machiavellian separation of politics from morality: Morality becomes a personal matter of the sovereign individual will and political (and, by extension) international relations become a matter of power. The modern state was the product of this conceptual shift away from the dominance of natural justice with the Christian prince as its enforcer.

Once the new system was in place (clearly by the seventeenth century), it then became easy to argue that the *cause* of war and international strife was the propensity of states to meddle in each other's affairs. In other words, the primacy of the sovereign will that was replacing the idea of the common good in interpersonal relations was simply writ large on the international scene as absolute sovereignty. Once this shift had occurred, there was little choice but to legally reinforce the new arrangement.

In the twentieth century, absolute sovereignty has been continuously written into the Law of Nations: The Covenant of the League of Nations (1920), The Convention on the Duties and Rights of States in the Event of Civil Strife (1928), and the Montevideo Convention on the Rights and Duties of States (1933). Moreover, it seemed self-evident to policy makers that the catastrophic conflicts of this century often followed breaches of national sovereignty, breaches that were frequently disguised as interventions in aid of some beleaguered party. In response to this perceived danger, the framers of the UN Charter were careful to build absolute sovereignty into law. Article 2, Section 7 specifically forbids intervention by one state into the affairs of another except in cases of self-defense, where this is understood or defined as the violation of recognized international borders.

A simultaneous historical development further strengthened the idea of sovereignty. In the immediate postwar period, the legal principle of the self-determination of peoples was specifically applied to the colonial territories of the European powers. One effect of this was to provide a powerful disincentive to intervention. Ironically, the imperial system of the eighteenth and nineteenth centuries was one response to the international anarchy created by absolute sovereignty. But the prevailing ideology of the autonomous will plus the inability of the colonial powers to retain their possessions rendered imperialism a temporary phenomenon. As a result, the theory of self-determination reached a peak in the 1960s. As a rubric for decolonization, the principle of self-determination could only reinforce absolute sovereignty.

Supplementing these political developments were the moral arguments, principally of the sort advanced by Walzer as discussed above, which claim that in a world of sovereign states, nonintervention is a precondition of the full exercise of self-determination (i.e., in a world in which the autonomous will is definitive of morality, the territorial integrity of the state is the final guarantee of rights).

And yet, these arguments are flawed because they are in conflict with the basic human goods. Or, at the least, the legalistic understanding of sovereignty must be conditioned by the idea of the good. This point is clearly made in a recent report of the Wilton Park Conference on the United Nations in the New World Disorder. The conference brought together an array of senior diplomats, policy makers, and academics. Commenting on the United Nations' support for a policy of nonintervention, the report states:

> However, Article 2 (7) is flawed because it sacrifices the cause of justice for peace. If strictly observed, it would bar any thought of exerting pressure on a tyrant, no matter how ghastly the crimes he was inflicting on his people, because his sovereignty was absolute within the frontiers of his state. But in the New World Disorder, the boundaries between domestic and international affairs is becoming more blurred, making it difficult to ascertain where the domestic affairs of a state end and the international domain begins.
>
> The view now prevailing is that the observance of fundamental human rights know no national boundaries and therefore should no longer be disregarded on account of state sovereignty. In early international law, when waging war was not outlawed, intervention was seen as a measure short of war. The assumption was that if a state could legally wage war, then it could intervene in a more limited way, including on humanitarian grounds. Intervention by a state in the internal affairs of another state seemed to have been warranted when its own citizens or the citizens of the state subjected to intervention were mistreated in a way inconsistent with civilized behavior.

As demonstrated by support for intervention in Northern Iraq, Somalia, Liberia and in former Yugoslavia, there is a fundamental shift in
international public opinion in favor of intervention on humanitarian
grounds and a stronger commitment to protection of human rights. UN
Resolution 688 stated that people in distress and in dire need have the
right of access to humanitarian assistance. Resolution 43/131 urged
"states in proximity to areas of natural disasters . . . to participate closely with the affected countries in international efforts with a view to
facilitating to the extent possible the transit of humanitarian assistance.
Resolution 45/182 called for humanitarian corridors. These resolutions
build upon the 1949 Geneva Conventions which recognize the right to
humanitarian assistance, although its exercise had previously been predicated on the consent of the state concerned. However, lately the Security Council has asserted the right of humanitarian access in Bosnia,
Iraq, and Somalia. Such access, with or without permission of the State
concerned, cannot today be construed as intervention in the affairs of
states.[9]

This quotation is typical of many such contemporary deliverances, statements that reflect a remarkable weakening of the doctrine
of nonintervention. Also typical here is the "two-story" approach.
The first level is a moral argument: "However, article 2 (7) is flawed
because it sacrifices justice for peace." In other words, the principles of natural justice supersede the Hobbesian/Machiavellian imperative to seek peace at all costs, even if this means tolerating an
oppressive and murderous sovereignty. The first signs of a revival
of the classical perspective of natural justice is also, necessarily, a
revival of the just-war tradition, for it is in terms of discriminate
and proportionate force only that interventions can be framed.

The second story of the two-story approach focuses on changed
political circumstances, specifically the deterioration of absolute
sovereignty as a result of the continuing emergence of a truly global community. While this in no way detracts from the importance
of particular cultural perspectives, it does portend a weakening of
political boundaries understood as inviolable. The argument here is
twofold. First, the cold war order has collapsed and with it the sharp
lines between domestic and foreign realms. Obviously, these are not
obliterated, but the overwhelming weight of traditional international law in support of absolute sovereignty has dramatically declined,
thus bringing *jus gentium* in closer accord with traditional theories
of *bellum justum* and with theories of natural justice. Second, the
weakening of sovereignty is itself a threat to peace. "A landmark
Presidential Statement (doc. s/24111, 1992) in the Security Council
observed that "non-military sources of instability in the economic,

humanitarian and ecological fields have become threats to peace and security." [10]

This argument highlights the pragmatic dimension of humanitarian intervention. The danger to world peace constituted by sustained human and ecological misery is obvious. If the "global village" concept has any validity at the level, at least of commerce and advanced communications, then the traditional view of purely "international affairs" will be much diminished. This argument is interesting precisely because it reverses the traditional reasons for nonintervention. On that argument, the cause of war is the interference of states in the internal matters of other states, while on the new view, it is the failure to do so (in restricted situations) that is the cause of war.

The Wilton Park Report concludes with a summary definition of the criteria for humanitarian intervention that seems to follow closely the view of Walzer: "It appears that a custom has been or is in the process of being developed, on the basis of which humanitarian intervention is justifiable whenever, for lack of an effective government, a country slides into anarchy, thus jeopardizing seriously the lives, security and well-being of the people. It is therefore generally accepted by governments, non-governmental organizations (NGOs) and the public that the international community should not allow people whose country is plunged in chaos, as in Somalia and in Liberia, to be killed indiscriminately or to be subjected to massive and systematic human rights abuses by their government." [11]

I conclude this section by analyzing the report's seven-point criteria for humanitarian intervention (pp. 8-9).

1. It should be undertaken by the UN, or on its mandate and under its authority and coordination, and/or by the regional organization to which the state belongs, so as to secure international control and legitimacy. There are steadily growing objections to the insistence that alternatives be exhausted before force is considered.

This provision wisely restricts the use of force to multinational organizations, the UN having the prime mandate as representing the global community. However, if there are regional associations with a more intimate and knowledgeable link to the conflict in question, such associations might be more appropriate means of intervention. There is also here the suggestion that the last-resort provision of *jus ad bellum* be more "realistically" interpreted. I take it that this is not intended as a "wink" at last-resort but a reminder not to slip into pacifism by default. In any event, the last-resort provision was never intended as requiring a *sequence* of nonbellicose stages leading up to the use for force. For example, some circumstances (such as a direct attack) would require force as the *first* step, even though this step would *be* the last resort.

2. When carried out by a regional organization concerned, it should be preceded by consultations with the security council.

Again, this is essentially a prudential matter, providing a system of checks and balances to maximize impartiality. Just as an individual is not a good judge in his own case, so a nation and, possibly, even a regional alliance.

3. It should be undertaken whenever there is a total lack of governmental institutions and the seriousness and the gravity of the humanitarian situation is such that the lives and well-being of the population as a whole is threatened. Intervention becomes a far more sensitive and a less practical proposition in cases where the country is still controlled by the government, although the lives and well-being of the population, or part of it, might be seriously threatened or might have been exposed to systematic and massive abuses by their government.

Clearly, if sovereignty has *totally* collapsed, there can be no violation of sovereignty. Intervention under these circumstances would be to rescue people from a state of nature and hardly even to be described as intervention at all. So the key question here is whether intervention is justifiable under conditions of greatly reduced or attenuated sovereignty. In short, is the key issue the degree of sovereignty or the degree of injustice or some combination of the two? According to the report's guidelines, decreasing levels of sovereignty do not rule out humanitarian intervention, but make it "problematic."

4. It should be proportionate in the sense that it should not cause more damage and harm than that caused by the situation it intends to correct.

This is a restatement of the *jus in bello* principle of proportionality: The right to use force is not unlimited even if the cause be morally justified. States are not permitted to use force in excess of the threat to themselves and to those whom they are charged to protect. The principle is at once a moral principle and a deliverance of prudence. Morally, force can only harm the good of human life and, prudentially, the use of force must be in pursuit of some political goal, thus ruling out a use of force that would likely undermine the policy goals themselves. In the case of limited political goals (as are necessarily embodied in the very idea of humanitarian intervention), proportionality becomes a guiding principle of prudence. Disproportionate force is likely to be counterproductive.

5. *It should not, in any way, interfere, influence, act against, or put into question the political independence and territorial integrity of the state concerned. At the same time, it should follow a strictly neutral approach in the sense that it should not attempt to take sides in the internal political conflict.*

This is clearly the most controversial and, indeed, ambiguous of the seven principles adopted by the report and it will be necessary to analyze it more fully below. For now, we can say that it is entirely unrealistic to suppose that an intervention, labeled "humanitarian" or otherwise, should not in *any way* condition the political independence and/or territorial integrity of the state concerned. Similarly, it is hardly likely that *strict* political neutrality is possible either, given that the genesis of humanitarian intervention is typically human suffering occasioned by political conflict.

6. *It should be limited in time and space.*

As with point 4, this is a restatement of just-war provisions. Ethically acceptable use of force must be limited in the sense of being proportionate and discriminate. Intervention must have clear and specific goals along with timetables and appropriate restraints on force levels. Traditional military concepts of defeat and victory (or winning and losing) are not meaningful in the context of humanitarian intervention. Pragmatically, this is certainly the most difficult provision to implement. As Clausewitz reminds us, force has an internal dynamic that tends to push it to an extreme. Military commanders in pursuit of their missions will necessarily seek to pacify, secure, and dominate ever-larger perimeters and sectors of territory and population. By nature aggressive and optimistic, they will also not be daunted by reverses and will seek to "press on regardless." These admirable qualities, which their training reinforces, are in some tension with the idea of limited military operations. When this is taken in conjunction with the expectations of modern democratic populations that wars will be decisive in outcome, we have a recipe for trouble. Forces earmarked for humanitarian intervention will require long-term special training in these types of operation. Officers with the appropriate temperament and intelligence should be identified and their talents utilized in command roles.

We look to Clausewitz for another reminder regarding what he called "friction." While war naturally tends toward the maximum expenditure of force (i.e., there are no restraints internal to war itself), yet the specific material and political conditions will exert some drag or "friction" on military operations. This phenomenon equally applies to timetables. History of warfare repeatedly shows that prewar timetables are always radically altered once combat commences. It is thus of critical importance that the civilian population be made fully aware of the rationale (both ethical and prudential) behind a policy of just intervention *and* of the tentative nature of strategic planning that structures such events, particularly the stipulation of precise timetables and schedules for withdrawal. As in war, the unforeseen arises more often than not, it is well to prepare civilians for this possibility.

In short, the requirement of limited, discriminate, and proportional use of force can only be realized in a democracy if humanitarian intervention is clearly articulated as a *national policy. Ad hoc* expeditions inspired by journalistic emotivism will merely generate domestic controversy, making a bipartisan approach much more difficult. The United States, and its allies, must decide through open discussion what is to count as humanitarian intervention and whether such use of force is appropriate as a mission of the state.

7. In situations of anarchy, where there is a total lack of government and no other governmental institutions are in place, it might also prove to be necessary to include in its objectives the promotion of (and assistance in) the political harmonization of the country, without taking sides in the political conflict.

This provision stipulates a degree of political involvement under limited circumstances (total anarchy). Here again, grave questions arise regarding the possibility of political restructuring ("harmonization") without taking sides in the political conflict, for if there is "total" anarchy, there is no "political" conflict at all.

The Wilton Park proposals are thus typical of many public policy statements favorable to what is claimed as an emerging consensus on humanitarian intervention. It clearly reflects all the strengths, weaknesses, and ambiguities of this position. On the positive side, humanitarian intervention seeks to conform international relations more fully to traditional conceptions of natural justice and, thus, to break the stranglehold of absolute sovereignty. As the report puts it:

> Thus a customary right of access to basic humanitarian needs mentioned in the Universal Declaration of Human Rights seems to have been formed which imposes a corresponding obligation on states: "there can (now) be no doubt that the provision of strictly humanitarian aid to persons or forces in another country, whatever their political affiliations or objectives, cannot be regarded as unlawful intervention, or as in any other way contrary to international law." Today the dialogue is no longer at the level of legal principles but of pragmatism. It is not a question of whether the international community has the right to intervene or whether it should intervene: it is a question of how and in what way. The issue is no longer whether humanitarian aid is intervention, but whether faced with the refusal of a state to allow access to humanitarian assistance, contrary to their obligation to do so, force can be used on humanitarian grounds.[12]

At the same time, the principle of humanitarian intervention is circumscribed in a way that seeks to limit drastically the scope of just intervention by scrupulously respecting state sovereignty. That is, under specific circumstances, we are morally required to ignore sovereignty when lives and rights, as specified in the UN Declaration of Human Rights, are denied. Apparently, the *mere abrogation* of these rights is insufficient to trigger humanitarian intervention. Rather, intervention only occurs when "a country slides into anarchy" and is unable to protect the lives, security, and well-being of its people.

Now, the first thing to notice here is the ambiguity of "anarchy." If anarchy is equivalent to a Hobbesian state of nature, then humanitarian intervention would seek to repair evils of omission. If there is no government, then the inhabitants of a specific territory are just being given the protection of civil society by the intervening power. Such an act seems morally uncontroversial, but where are such examples to be found?

On the other hand, actual cases mentioned in the report (Somalia and Liberia) involve not so much anarchy as governments oppressing their own people. Here, we have not so much a state of

nature as a civil war. In these cases, it is not easy to distill the
essence of the humanitarian from the political. It is perhaps this
abstraction of man, or the human, from the *polis* that renders problematical and controversial this formulation of humanitarian intervention. This returns us to the starting point of our reflections: There
is indeed a common human nature ordained toward the basic human goods. But human beings are always found realizing these
goods within some *polis*. This *polis* is not some sort of add-on to
their humanity (for community itself is one of the basic human
goods), but is the form through which the fundamental questions of
life are articulated. It is, therefore, necessary to delineate more precisely the idea of the humanitarian. The crucial question is this: Can
the moral imperative to protect human rights and life be separated
from the political context in which these rights are to be exercised?
To put this another way: Having once breached the barrier of nonintervention in the cause of human rights, may we stop short of full
political guarantees of these rights?

The most perceptive critic of theories of humanitarian intervention is Hadley Arkes. In *First Things*, Arkes begins by analyzing
the antiwar opposition to American intervention in Vietnam. The
wrongfulness of the war in Vietnam, it was argued, turned on the
right of the people of that country to self-determination. What was
important was that they be permitted to struggle and to determine
their own fate *even if* the result turned out not to be a democratic
regime. The United States had no right to "impose" upon the Viet-
namese a regime of representative democracy. This is the basis, as
we have seen, of Michael Walzer's objection to the U.S. presence
in Vietnam. The criterion for intervention in a situation of civil war
is the test of self-help: Can the government we propose to aid command the loyalty of its people? "A government that receives economic and technical aid, military supply, strategic and tactical
advice, and is still unable to reduce its subjects to obedience, is
clearly an illegitimate government . . . The Saigon regime was so
much an American creature that the U.S. government's claim to be
committed to it and obligated to ensure its survival is hard to understand." [13]

But as Arkes points out, these premises of Walzer have no *moral* significance: "It is entirely possible that elected governments with
the support of their population may still not be a match, in certain
instances, for terrorist groups that are disciplined and unconstrained
by tender sentiments. Certain populations may also be demoralized

or lose their nerve more easily than others when they are faced with systematic terror, and they may be more inclined to buy peace by accepting an accommodation, even with antidemocratic forces. But it should be apparent at the same time that nothing in this catalogue of weakness would affect in any way the *moral* claim of an elected government to survive that terrorism. And in that event, as I think I have shown, the canons of moral reasoning would explain quite easily why a third party would be justified in going to the rescue and supplying the strength that the endangered government cannot summon by itself. Against the necessary force of these moral considerations, the doctrine of nonintervention must be reduced to a formula without moral substance." [14]

For Walzer (as for the peace movement), the proper working out of self-determination precludes the type of assistance provided by the United States to the government of South Vietnam on the grounds that this government had failed the test of self-help, *even when* it was clear that the denial of such help would certainly subject the people of South Vietnam to massive suppression of their rights. In support of this point, Arkes notes that in the spring of 1977, within two years of the fall of Saigon, an "Appeal to the Government of Vietnam" was signed by Joan Baez, Staughton Lynd, Aryeh Neier, and many other activists in the antiwar movement. The appeal charged that the new government of Vietnam had imposed upon the people of South Vietnam a despotism involving "grievous and systematic violations of human rights by your government." Arkes argues that by resting its appeal on the notion of universal human rights, the antiwar movement necessarily undermines its previous argument for nonintervention. For if there is a moral imperative to protect human rights, how can we deny those same people the political means to sustain their rights in the form of political institutions?

> In other words, how could one insist on a vast body of legal rights for human beings without insisting at the same time on the creation of "a government of law?" And how could one insist on the institutions of a legal order without recognizing that the same premises which enjoin government by law also enjoin government by consent and a regime of free elections? [15]

Hence, if a people are being oppressed, their right to relief surely does not depend upon whether they possess the strength or the wit to defend their own interests. To abandon them to tyranny on *those* grounds (albeit dressed up in the principles of self-determination and nonintervention) is simply to fail to take human rights seriously; to substitute prudence for morality.

> And yet the activists might not have been deluded in that way. They might have simply thought it possible that the "human rights" they esteemed could indeed be detached from the structure of constitutional government. But it should be evident that if they had understood the connection between human rights and constitutional government, they would have understood from the beginning the principles that were engaged in the war in Vietnam. If they understood why it was proper for themselves in 1977 to speak across the ocean to another culture and expect the government of Vietnam to honor certain requirements of justice, then they would have understood why it was legitimate for the United States in the 1960s to weigh the prospect of a totalitarian regime in South Vietnam and find it to be quite as undesirable in principle in Asia as it was in America. And if there were grounds on which the United States could indeed judge what was better or worse in principle for the people of another country, then the so-called principle of nonintervention would be exposed for what it has ever been: a rule of prudence in international affairs, but hardly a proposition that bears the moral substance of a genuine principle.[16]

If the principle on nonintervention lacks moral substance, then it is impossible to frame a moral argument for the protection of human life and rights that, in principle, may be detached from political reform. I believe this argument to be sound and to thus have clear implications for theories of humanitarian intervention. In light of this, it appears that humanitarian intervention represents a genuine effort to enshrine the protection of human rights in international law while retaining the principle of sovereignty or nonintervention in a fairly strong form. The ambiguities and lack of clear criteria for such intervention reflect this inherent conflict, a conflict that is papered over by attempting to isolate human rights from a political and historical context.

> It may be no surprise that the same principle would stand behind the argument, often made today, that the United States is obliged to go to the rescue of the hungry of the world. Ironically, the people who make this argument are willing to contemplate an intervention in the politics of another country if that were necessary to the humanitarian mission of bringing food to the starving. Without such awareness, the spokesmen for this persuasion have themselves absorbed Hobbesian premises: they assume that the preservation of life is a purpose which must override all others and transcend political differences. Paradoxically then,

they would blind themselves to the question of whether the lives they would save are imprisoned, in effect, in regimes that are despotic and murderous, and whether the aid they would render would actually work to strengthen those regimes. The question, in that event, is whether the principle that enjoins an obligation to rescue would entail a commitment to do far more than preserve the lives of the victims. Might we also not be obliged to deliver people, where we can, from regimes of oppression, and establish the kinds of government that are more fitting by nature for human beings.[17]

We are now in a position to understand the essential lack of coherence as exemplified in, for example, the Wilton Park Report. For it is only by abstracting from the totality of man-in-community the value of life and rights and construing them as a separate "humanitarian" category that it is possible to sustain a proposal to intervene while, at the same time, strictly avoiding political involvement.

Humanitarian Intervention: A First Step

A conclusive moral assessment of humanitarian intervention is problematic due to the continuing evolution of the practice. Clearly, there is a shift taking place in international law and in the practice of nations regarding this kind of intervention. Whether public opinion has kept up with these developments is less clear. However, at some point, the unresolved tensions inherent in humanitarian intervention will have to be faced. There appears to have emerged two formulations of humanitarian intervention. The first is an unrestricted form, wherein all institutions of civil order have broken down, anarchy reigns, and the inhabitants suffer loss of rights and life due to the absence of civil society. In cases such as these, there seems little doubt that intervention that has as its goal the restoration of civil order could be anything but morally required. There would be no point whatever in rescuing people from starvation and disease simply to abandon them to a state of nature *or* to the form of government that led them into anarchy in the first place. Of course, immense practical difficulties may limit what anyone may accomplish but, in principle, something that calls itself humanitarian intervention must at the least *presuppose* the right to endow such people with representative government. There must be no double-talk or diplomatic "waffling" on this matter, as appears in Article 7

of the Wilton Park Report, which speaks of the need to produce
". . . political harmonization of the country without taking sides in
the political conflict." Humanitarian intervention backed by such
vagueness will likely produce inconsequential results. In any event,
where are there actual instances of populations with a "total lack
of governmental institutions?" Certainly, none of the current list of
candidates for humanitarian intervention fits this description. Somalia, Bosnia, Haiti, and Rwanda all fall under a second category of
humanitarian intervention, the restricted. In these cases, there are
active political units competing for control with territory and institutions of government or, as in the case of Haiti, there is an oppressive regime in power bringing death and destruction upon its
people. In this sort of case, it seems clear that exhortations to follow "a strictly neutral approach" vis-à-vis the political regime makes
little moral, prudential, or tactical sense. Here again, it would be
morally retrograde to bring someone back from the brink of death
only to resubmit him to the political regime whose ineptness or
malice consigned him to starvation in the first place. For *unless* one
adopts the extreme Hobbesian position that physical survival is the
supreme, overriding human good, there must be a link between the
humanitarian impulse to save lives and the further provision of a
political regime that will safeguard life and rights.

Humanitarian intervention is, thus, a *first step* in the right direction insofar as it recognizes that the classical principles of nonintervention and absolute sovereignty must give way on those
occasions when, in the words of classical just-war theory, "an injustice goes uncorrected in another place." The *next step* should be
the logical unfolding of an expanded theory of humanitarian intervention, which will mandate political reform where necessary and
practically possible as morally inseparable from the duty of charity. Without such a commitment, efforts to help starving and oppressed peoples will be operationally self-stultifying and morally
incoherent.

Notes

1. John Paul II, *Centesimus Annus* (Washington, D.C.: United States Catholic Council, 1991) 46.

2. Augustine, *The City of God* (New York, N.Y.: Image Books, 1958),
301.

3. Nicolo Machiavelli, *The Prince* (New York, N.Y.: Mentor, 1952), 94.

4. Michael Walzer, *Just and Unjust Wars* (New York, N.Y.: Basic Books, 1977), 89.

5. Ibid, 90.

6. Ibid, 87.

7. Ibid, 106.

8. Ibid, 105.

9. Nicholas Hopkinson, *The United Nations in the New World Disorder* (London: Her Majesty's Stationery Office, 1993), 5.

10. Ibid, 6.

11. Ibid, 7.

12. Ibid, 6 (Article 70, paragraph 2, Geneva Protocol I, 1978).

13. Hadley Arkes, *First Things* (Princeton, N.J.: Princeton University Press, 1986), 98.

14. Ibid, 13.

15. Ibid, 263.

16. Ibid, 264.

17. Ibid, 287.

Pacifist Perspectives on Humanitarian Intervention

Introduction

The judgments we make in this world are influenced by a great many "givens"—that is, by beliefs, values, assumptions, and attitudes so much a part of our outlooks that we simply take them for granted. A philosophic consideration of any value position should make explicit as many of these factors as possible so that our value judgments involve full awareness of initial conditions, including values and predispositions embedded in the conceptual frameworks that may shape or otherwise influence our reflections. Beyond making "givens" explicit, a philosophic examination of issues calling for value judgments should clarify concepts crucial to those judgments. Humanitarian intervention is a complex and often confusing notion in need of just such philosophical reflection.

The modern world consists of some 178 (or so) nations, each claiming political sovereignty and territorial integrity over particular parcels of land. Whenever one nation imposes itself within the boundaries of another, we have intervention. Such impositions often involve deployment of military personnel and equipment and typically aim at specific goals, goals sufficiently important to the intervening nation to risk injury and death as well as the reactions of other interested nations. Interventions are called "humanitarian" in an effort to explain and justify nations' suspension of the usual respect for the boundaries of other nations. Humanitarian interventions are claimed to be morally acceptable despite the violation of boundaries because the good to be achieved by the intervention somehow outweighs the wrong of suspending the usual respect for borders.

Military intervention is the focus of the following discussion, yet it is important to recognize a pervasive activity akin to intervention, usually taken for granted as humanitarian, which in itself is not military. Dominant nations often undertake to "develop" the world outside their own borders through corporate investment, marketing, access to natural resources, and employment of indigenous labor, typically imposing dominant culture values and institutions in the process. Most such efforts have, at best, mixed goals, often seeking significant economic, political, or other advantage for the developers as well as economic expansion for the developing nation. This quieter, less explicitly invasive relative of intervention frequently precedes and often helps explain the alleged necessity of subsequent military interventions, since many of the latter are undertaken to protect corporate interests, employees and property. More will be said about such "developmentalism"[1] later in this discussion.

The concept of humanitarian intervention arises not only within a global arena consisting of multiple independent sovereign nations but also within a dominant value tradition concerning the morality of war. Conventional wisdom reveals three distinct positions: 1) war realism, which considers morality irrelevant to war; 2) the just-war tradition, which offers guidelines for the moral acceptability of war; and 3) pacifism, which regards war to be morally wrong. When conventional wisdom is extended to cover military intervention, we find that war realism requires no moral justification for intervention, that intervention may or may not be justified for *just-warism*, and that intervention cannot be justified for pacifism. Clearly the dominant value tradition embraces the just-warist perspective on intervention.

Consideration of pacifist perspectives on humanitarian intervention must begin within this context. Pacifists are few and often are taken to be well-meaning but naive, morally upright but unrealistic, insufficiently pragmatic, idealistic in the extreme. Rarely is pacifism taken seriously, especially when it comes to international issues.

While the purpose of this essay is to examine pacifist perspectives on humanitarian intervention, much of what is needed to do so involves examination and critique of the "givens" mentioned above. Pacifism is a complex and subtle range of value positions on morality, peace, and war, not the stereotyped extreme of conventional wisdom. The varieties of pacifism have emerged within a just-warist value tradition, to some degree building on and extending that tradition. So, before a pacifist position on humanitarian intervention can be made explicit, pacifism and its relation to just-warism needs to be considered.

In what follows I begin with an examination of the dominant value perspective, review the principles and varieties of just-warism, describe the range of pacifist views, and establish a context for the moral assessment of intervention as it occurs today. A pacifist critique of military intervention is developed prior to concluding this exploration of pacifist perspectives on humanitarian intervention with often neglected alternatives including nonviolent intervention. As we will see, there is no single pacifist position concerning humanitarian intervention. Rather, there is a rich and varied range of views, not all mutually compatible but all in broad agreement that modern nations tend to be overly self-interested in coming to judgment on the legitimacy of intervention, too quick to resort to military means, and uninterested in the development and application of truly humane, nonviolent peacemaking.

✕ Warism

Warism is the view that war is morally justifiable in principle and often morally justified in fact. Although warism is expressed in various ways, from warist language to warist behavior, the central notion is that war is morally acceptable, largely because it is a simple fact of nature.

All cultures have basic concepts, values, assumptions, and beliefs that together form a frame of reference or conceptual scheme through which members of the culture experience the world. Conceptual schemes consist in what is taken as "given" when engaging the world. Regarding values, the effect is as if a culture's members were wearing normative lenses through which "reality" is conceived and appraised.

For most of the modern world, warism is an unconscious predisposition. It seems so obvious to the vast majority of people that war is morally acceptable that they do not realize they are assuming it; no other way of understanding large-scale human conflict has occurred to them. In this sense warism is like racism, sexism, and homophobia: a prejudicial bias built in to conceptions and judgments without the awareness of those presupposing it.

In another form, warism is explicitly held, openly articulated, and deliberately chosen as a value judgment on nations in conflict. In its implicit form, warism is an uncritical presumption that distorts judgments and leads warists to take war to be a perfectly normal, natural, and even necessary element of international relations. In its explicit form, war is openly defended as "the only thing the enemy understands," brandished as a threat to secure the status quo or carefully justified as essential to justice. In both forms warism misguides judgments and institutions; it reinforces the necessity and inevitability of war by precluding alternatives.

Evidence abounds to support the notion that warism is a dominant contemporary outlook. In virtually every aspect of society—politics, education, entertainment, business, sports, even religion and interpersonal relations—conflicts entail contests for superiority. Politicians indicate seriousness about problems by declaring wars: on poverty, on drugs, on illiteracy, on crime. Professional athletes no longer strive merely to outdo opponents in the skills of a given sport and win games; now athletes must dominate, even humiliate, opponents with an "in your face" arrogance. Big games are battles; championships are wars. Even scholars are embattled. Their combat takes the form of verbal attack and rejoinder, fighting for truth, exchanging linguistic blows in efforts to win arguments, defeat rivals, and prevail. While every schoolchild learns the battles, tactics, and heroics of wars that gave us the current configurations of both the political globe and the domestic agenda, nonviolent leaders of cooperative and collaborative rather than domineering policies are largely ignored.

Perhaps the most significant indicator that warism is our dominant paradigm is the fact that the burden of justification concerning value judgments of conflict rests on pacifists, not warists. The war system—the standard operating procedure of nations constantly preparing for, threatening, and undertaking war—is simply taken for granted. The burden of proof rests on anyone challenging the paradigm. With the warist conceptual framework in the dominant position, moral considerations of war turn to questions of the moral acceptability of a particular war or of specific acts within a given war. While these are important issues, focusing on them leaves unchallenged the presumption that war itself is justifiable.

The slow but persistent rise of awareness within the dominant culture of racial, ethnic, and gender oppression and the efforts for liberation by members of oppressed groups offer hope that even the most deeply entrenched and least challenged presumptions of life might be examined and criticized. Although largely marginalized and often dismissed, criticisms of the dominant war paradigm—of warism—may follow the course of racial, ethnic, gender, affectional-orientation, and other progressive rights-advocacy movements to a point when war is no longer taken for granted as natural, moral, and inevitable. Perhaps one day warists rather than pacifists will be expected to bear the primary burden of justifying their views, and nonviolent alternatives for resolving conflict will be routinely taught and widely known rather than exceptional. Recognizing warism is a first step to such a future.

Explorations of pacifist perspectives on humanitarian intervention take place within a warist context. Recognizing the prejudicial dominant conceptual scheme opens the possibility of a fair consideration of otherwise neglected options.

⨯ Just-Warism

The concept of just war has been a part of Western culture at least as far back as the written record takes us. Accounts of war invariably include efforts to explain, defend, condone, or otherwise justify warmaking. Groups seem virtually incapable of mass armed violence in the absence of reasons for seeing their efforts to be in the right while questioning the morality of their enemies.

Western culture has a long tradition of expecting and providing moral justifications for war and acts within wars, despite the lack of clearly universal value standards on which to base such judgments. To this day there is wide disagreement on who should decide the morality of war and on the appropriate grounds for their decisions. Although some scholars make reference to "the just-war theory," it seems more accurate to refer to a just-war *tradition.* There is no single precise and explicit doctrine or document of any government, treaty, church, international body, or moral theory that qualifies as "the just-war theory." Rather, we have generally accepted but variously interpreted guidelines about morality and war that have arisen in numerous ways and have been evolving for centuries. Sources are varied: broad cultural values, narrowly religious and military elements, ancient philosophic and literary texts, contemporary military codes of conduct, and so on.

War realism seems to have been among the early dominant views on war. It is the view that war occurs outside of morality. War is just a natural activity, a fact of nature. When war happens the best thing to do is set aside moral considerations and win; there will be time for morality afterward. "All's fair in love and war" captures the war realist's inclination to exempt war from ordinary moral standards, and to justify doing so on moral grounds.

The just-war tradition emerges as a reaction to war realism, perhaps out of self-interest, or through recognizing the suffering of victims on all sides, or perhaps out of moral concern for the effects of warmaking on the character of warmakers themselves. Accounts of varying degrees of moral restraint in the conduct of war are recorded in such ancient texts as Homer's *Iliad* and Plato's *Republic*. After the ancient Greek city-states were consolidated through conquest by Alexander, they were absorbed by the Roman Empire into an even wider military domination including the Mediterranean world and Europe. From the end of the second century until the fall of Imperial Rome at the close of the fifth, the empire was constantly at war. Despite Roman persecution, the early Christian Church was pacifistic to the point of nonresistance. But with Emperor Constantine's conversion to Christianity in 313, church and state united in embracing the notion of just war.

Augustine's teachings on war, developed near the start of the fifth century, guided the church and continue to shape the tradition. Derived from the ancient principles of Plato and Cicero but with Christian additions, Augustine's view allows killing to be compatible with Christian love. This is because spiritual salvation is taken to be more important than the life of the body, and because attitudes, not actions, determine right and wrong. With the right intent, war may vindicate justice; if atrocities are avoided, war can create peace. Just as Augustine built upon earlier values, so Augustine's principles have been refined, extended, and amended into the broad guidelines of current just-war values.

The just-war tradition has evolved around two distinct but related themes: 1) the *jus ad bellum* or moral justification for going *to* war and 2) the *jus in bello* or moral guidelines for conduct *within* war. Each requires specific conditions to be met.[2] For a war to be just it must be both morally justified to undertake and morally conducted once undertaken. The tradition itself is conceived largely along a domestic analogy. That is, states or nations are taken as rough moral equivalents to individual persons. So, if a person is justified in defending her- or himself from an unprovoked attacker, then a nation is as well; if a person may intervene on behalf of another suffering unjust abuse, then a nation may as well.

The moral justification for going to war—the *jus ad bellum*—is often described to involve six distinct conditions: 1) only a *just cause* warrants war; 2) only a *right authority* may make the decision to go to war; 3) groups going to war may do so only with *right intention*; that is, to right a wrong and bring about peace, never intending revenge, harm, or self-interest; 4) war may be undertaken only as a *last resort* and only if the goal is 5) a *likely emergent peace*; finally, 6) the war may not be *disproportionate*, that is, the total evil of a just war may not outweigh the good achieved by the war. Each of these six conditions must be met independently for a group or nation to go to war justly. The tradition presumes a moral abhorrence of war but allows war when the conditions are met.

Since this examination of the just-war tradition is to provide a context for understanding the pacifist tradition, the purpose is not to develop just-warism in all its detail. But since pacifism urges greater moral restraint than just-warism requires, and since it does so in part through objections to just war both in principle and in application, a bit more development is needed here.

Perhaps the feature of the *jus ad bellum* aspect of the just war tradition most crucial to intervention is the notion of *just cause*. The basic principle of the just-cause requirement is that aggression is a crime and that war is justly undertaken only in response to aggression. Aggression is a threat or use of force by one state against the political sovereignty or territorial integrity of another. Self-defense is the fundamental rationale for going to war, but the principle of just cause extends to include defense of other states against aggression as well as interventions to assist secessionists, to balance other interventions, and to protect potential victims from egregious human rights violations such as enslavement and massacre. The just cause principle has been used to justify even preemptive strikes against potential aggressors.[3]

Deciding when it is just to go to war is a complex and difficult task. When a war of intervention is under consideration, the decision is especially problematic. This is because aggression is always a crime from the just-warist perspective. Since every intervention involves suspension of usual standards regarding respect for sovereignty and territorial integrity, every intervention risks being seen as aggression. Interventions are therefore exceptions to the general rules of the just-war tradition. Justified interventions are exceptions allowed under special rules.

Whenever a general system of rules allows suspension of those rules under special circumstances the system itself is vulnerable concerning its credibility. The complexity and subtlety of just-war guidelines and the exceptions regarding intervention, when conjoined with the political, economic, and strategic interests of involved nations, result in questionable interpretations and applications of value standards. The just-war tradition is not a fixed formula into which one can plug empirical factors for a given situation and thus generate an unambiguous conclusion. Rather, it is a broad set of value guidelines that get variously interpreted and applied. This is partly due to the sheer complexity of issues, and partly to the mixed motives of interested parties. Concerning intervention, the credibility of the tradition is especially vulnerable because in addition to the usual complexities and mixed motives, the rules themselves allow for suspending their own general moral guidelines. So it is over cases of intervention that the just-war tradition is in its weakest position.

Even if the various conditions required by the *jus ad bellum* were unambiguously satisfied in a given case, still the *jus in bello* conditions must be met. That is, even if a nation is justified in going to war, that war is not just unless it is conducted within the just-war guidelines. This second aspect of just war, moral conduct within war, has three basic principles: 1) *discrimination* or the immunity of innocents as governed by 2) *double effect*, distinguishing intended from unintended results, and 3) *proportionality*, here referring to specific acts within war rather than to the overall proportionality considerations of *jus ad bellum* mentioned above. Regardless of how just it may be for a nation to go to war, if the war cannot be conducted within the *jus in bello* guidelines it is not a just war.

Again we find complexity and subtlety in interpreting and applying just-war conditions. If a war is justly fought, innocents have immunity. Innocents are understood to be those not contributing to the war effort: children, the elderly, those hospitalized, and so on. Those conducting the war must discriminate between appropriate and inappropriate targets of the acts of war; it is always a war crime to target innocents. Certainly there are varying degrees of participation in the war effort, from engaging in combat to working in munitions factories and preparing supply needs for food and medicine.

Deciding who is innocent and thereby an inappropriate target is not a simple matter. Residential dwellings of ordinary people have traditionally enjoyed immunity, but modern warfare has reached into neighborhoods in efforts to break popular support for wars. Opinions differ on drawing the line between innocents and appropriate targets.

Even if innocence and immunity were clear and precise, the principle of *double effect* recognizes the inevitable "spillage" of war and thus excuses injury and death to innocents as long as such results are not intended. The just-war tradition distinguishes the intended effects on legitimate military targets from the unintended effects of injury or death to innocents (thus the name, "double effect"). While it is always wrong to target innocents, their victimization may be excused as unintended and is often explained as "collateral losses."

Proportionality guides conduct in war by disallowing specific acts or tactics if the good likely to be gained from them is insufficient to outweigh the evil of doing them. Put another way, the only acts allowed within the conduct of war must be acts with likely results good enough to compensate for the injury, death, and destruction they entail.

To be just, wars must meet both sets of conditions: they must be just to undertake and they must be justly fought. Clearly a war is not just if the rules of engagement are observed but the conditions for going to war are not met. And even if a nation is justified in going to war, if it cannot be conducted justly, then it is not a just war.

The discussions of proportionality as a feature of both *jus ad bellum* and *jus in bello* just-war conditions point to an important characteristic of the tradition. War is never seen as good in itself. Even to its proponents, war is evil. But, according to the just-war tradition, the evil of war may be necessary for good to prevail in the end. When war is morally chosen it is so not because it is good but because it is seen to be the least evil of available options. This indicates the just-war tradition to be predominantly consequentialist in its ethics.

There are a number of ways to conceptualize ethics in the Western intellectual tradition. Virtue ethics, characteristic of Classical Western philosophy as distinct from Modern,[4] conceives ethics to be a matter of character rather than of either duties or results. For Classical thinkers like Plato and Aristotle, being moral has to do with excelling in certain virtues, like courage and self-control. Modern ethics may be seen as broadly divided between teleological or ends-based ethics and deontological or duty-based ethics. Basing moral rightness on the likely consequences, the results, is teleological; basing moral rightness on obligation or duty is deontological. The ethics of care emergent within contemporary feminist philosophy turns from the Modern emphasis on duties, consequences, and rules for restraint of aggression, to focus instead on mutual interdependencies and a responsibility of care to meet human needs. The ethics of care is more akin to virtue ethics, yet avoids the preoccupation with rationality at the expense of emotion characteristic of Classical ethics. The Modern deontological/consequentialist framework seems the most helpful in understanding the arguments over morality and war, perhaps due to identifications of both Modern ethics and the just-war tradition with traditional notions of masculinity.

The just-war tradition focuses on ends to justify means. The acts of war are ordinarily wrong but they are allowed as necessary in response to aggression if the good they bring about offsets the evil they entail. This opens the just-war tradition to two different sorts of objections: critics might simply disagree and present counter evidence about the claim (in a specific case or in general) that the expected good outweighs the evil of war; or critics might reject the principle that evil means can be morally excused if they bring about good ends. As we will see, different sorts of pacifists take different positions on this issue.

Perhaps one last thing should be said about the just-war tradition in the way of background for development of a pacifist perspective on humanitarian intervention; it follows from much of what has been said above about just-war principles but it should be emphasized and clarified. Although proponents of just-warism agree that war is morally justifiable in principle and at least sometimes morally justified in fact, they need not agree on much else. That is, there are many versions or degrees of just-warism. This is inevitable for any tradition so old and so complex. After all, this tradition has evolved from disparate sources for over two thousand years and it continues to evolve as global events present themselves for moral consideration. It is not a straightforward doctrine with clear and measurable conditions that admit to objective empirical testing.

Individuals appealing to the tradition to justify—or to deny justification for—any particular war must interpret, select, and emphasize elements from within a complicated and interrelated set of guidelines. In doing so they weigh various aspects of the tradition differently. Some exploit the guidelines to rationalize doing whatever they have otherwise decided to do. Others meticulously consider the full set of conditions in an open investigation to discover the best moral course. Some emphasize the presumed abhorrence of war to exhaust every conceivable alternative. Others stress the crime of aggression and the right of intervention to reestablish justice. Always there are conflicting interests to complicate judgments. Always there are honest disagreements among proponents of just war. The result is a broad spectrum of positions on both the justifiability of war in principle and on the moral wisdom of applications to particular wars. While the tradition offers broad guidance to moral considerations of war, there are no easy answers. Individual people bear the burden of making moral judgments about war. The just-war tradition can help, but the responsibility belongs to each of us.

Varieties of Critical Pacifism

Pacifism is moral opposition to war and moral disposition toward cooperative personal, social, and national conduct based on agreement.[5] Pacifism embraces a wide range of positions from an absolute prohibition of all use of force at one extreme to a selective opposition to specific uses of force at the other. Pacifists disagree about the moral grounds for rejecting war, disagree about the moral acceptability of other forms of violence, and differ on their degrees of commitment to various forms of nonviolence.

"Pacifism" is the union of two ancient Latin words and literally means "peacemaking." Often pacifism is incorrectly taken to be "passivism," which comes from a different Latin root and means being inactive, accepting, and suffering. Pacifists may be passivists but more often are activists, choosing nonviolence to resolve conflict and create cooperative order.

There are two parts to pacifism. One is the opposition to war. This is the critical side of pacifism and is sometimes called "antiwar pacifism." Understanding the range of views within this aspect of pacifism rests upon grasping various objections to prevailing values concerning war, namely, objections to warism, war realism, and the just-war tradition. The second part of pacifism is sometimes called the "positive peace" aspect. It consists of a range of positions on peace as not merely the absence of war but as a positive condition of order that arises from within a group by cooperation among participants rather than order imposed from outside the group through domination by others. All pacifists accept some degree of both features of pacifism.

Although conventional wisdom tends to view war realism, just-warism, and pacifism as three distinct options on morality and war, the just-war and pacifist traditions have much in common. Both reject the war-realist claim that morality is irrelevant to war, and both adopt elaborate and varying conditions imposing moral restraint onto undertaking and conducting war. Just as one can envision degrees of just-warism based on the extent of moral restraint required in war, so one can envision degrees of pacifism where the moral restraint required prohibits war. Seeing the just-war and pacifist traditions linked along a single moral-restraint continuum respects a common value relationship without denying important points of contention. This opens discussion among adherents to both traditions and acknowledges complex and difficult differences of degree between them.

To begin with the critical aspect of pacifism, the most extreme form is *absolute pacifism*, which holds that it is wrong always and everywhere for anyone to use force against living things. This position has very few if any adherents, but some individuals aspire to such an ideal. A slightly weaker, near-absolute form of pacifism rests on a distinction between force and violence and allows some restrained forms of force but always rejects violence. This distinction is difficult but meaningful.

"Violence" is derived from a Latin word meaning "vehemence," which itself comes from Latin words meaning "to carry force." So violence literally means "intense force." It shares its etymology with "violate," which means "injury." So, violence refers to both extreme force (e.g., a violent storm or earthquake) and forced injury (e.g., rape, terrorism, or war).[6] Near-absolute pacifists allow some modest force but oppose all violence. This might mean accepting only nonviolent apprehension of criminals, for example. The force/violence distinction gets particularly tricky when increasing contemporary references to "institutional violence" are taken into consideration. This will receive a more deeply developed discussion later.

Further down the continuum moving away from absolute pacifism is *collectivist pacifism*, a position that opposes war yet allows some force, perhaps even lethal force, under restricted conditions. One may consistently object to war on moral grounds yet retain the right to defend oneself by force against unprovoked attack. The position taken regarding the morality of war need not dictate one's position on moral considerations of small-scale, interpersonal violence. Grasping collectivist pacifism helps us understand why large-scale, hard-to-control wars are easier for pacifists to condemn and more difficult for just-warists to support than are small-scale, well-controlled wars. This form of pacifism undercuts the just-warist tendency to use scale-reducing analogies in their defense of war.

As mentioned above, many just-war traditionalists model the moral guidelines for nations and war after broadly accepted moral standards concerning persons in conflict. Analogical reductionism often accompanies such thinking. Wars get described as "policing actions," even though the enemy is not apprehended for trial as is typical of policing. Bombing raids become "surgical strikes," although their precision hardly approaches that of medical operating procedures. These and other scale-reducing analogies are used to persuade oneself as well as others that a given act of war is morally acceptable. Collectivist pacifism rests on recognizing and taking into consideration the significance of scale in making moral judgments.

Still further along the continuum toward just-warism is the epistemological or *fallibility pacifist*, who concedes the moral justifiability of war in principle but denies it in fact. The crux of this reasoning is that even if it were possible to justify war in theory, to do so in practice would require a great deal more knowledge than those making the judgment in fact have. War is just too complicated with too many subtle and difficult implications for anyone to have confident knowledge of relevant factors sufficient to warrant large-scale destruction, injury, and death.

Technological pacifists also grant the justifiability of war in principle but their denial of moral justification in practice rests on the technology of modern war. War may have been morally justifiable centuries ago when volunteer participants met in remote battlefields with spears, but modern war has been altered by its own implements and has become insufficiently controllable. War "spills" beyond legitimate targets; the "front" can no longer be identified. Modern weapons threaten civilian populations without discrimination. Technological pacifists may differ on the precise conditions of or the era during which war became morally obsolete.

Nuclear pacifism is a contemporary subset of technological pacifism so named because of its focus on the role of nuclear weapons in forever changing the nature of war. Nuclear weapons possess so high a magnitude of destructive capacity with such uncontrollable effects that nuclear pacifists find their use unthinkable.

Ecological pacifism is another subset of technological pacifism. Noting that the military segment of our world is the leading contributor to global environmental pollution, ecological pacifists concentrate on the environmental impact not only of war but of research, development, testing, and deployment of the means of war, since all aspects of any warmaking capability risk disastrous consequences for sustainable ecosystems.

Pragmatic pacifism is at the weakest end of the pacifist continuum, alongside those just-warists imposing the most stringent moral restraint on war. Once again the argument turns not on abstract principles but empirical data. Some pragmatic pacifists reject virtually all wars on moral grounds based on the historical record. Despite the sincere convictions of many just-war proponents, wars rarely live up to their promise of creating peace and justice. Historical evidence supports the claim that wars contribute mightily to destruction of property as well as dislocation, suffering, injury, and death to millions of people. For pragmatic pacifists, war seems a poor risk, given the lessons of history.

Other pragmatic pacifists oppose a specific, selected war on moral grounds because it seems unlikely that it will yield the desired objectives. Some might think violence morally justifiable yet unwise because their own group happens to be outnumbered or outequipped. At this point there may well be overlap between the pacifist and just-warist traditions since the moral considerations are specific to given conditions and the weakest sort of pacifists may sometimes be persuaded of the justifiability of war just as the just-warists most stringent in their application of just-war moral restraint conditions may sometimes be convinced that war is wrong. This overlap reinforces the suggestion that the pacifist and just-war traditions differ more in degree than in kind.

It should be clear that there is much more to pacifism than the popular stereotype would suggest. Pacifists object to war for a variety of reasons and do not always agree, just as just-warists justify war in a variety of ways and are not always in agreement with one another. Despite the range of pacifist positions on the critical or "antiwar" aspect of pacifism, all pacifists agree that war is not an

inevitable and necessary fact of nature. Warists, especially war realists, often think that it is. Just-warists vary on this point, but are
inclined to see war as necessary in fact if not required in principle
by the natural order of things.

For pacifists, war is an elaborate institution created and sustained
culturally. This is why recognizing and challenging the warist bias-
es prevalent in dominant culture are so important. War may inevitably follow from particular conditions of injustice, exploitation,
wanton disregard for human rights, and so on, but such conditions
themselves are not necessary. Rather, they are merely contingent
features of life. Personal, social, and international relationships could
be arranged without persistent injustice, exploitation, and violations
of human rights. This realization leads to the second aspect of pacifism, the commitment to positive peace.

Varieties of Positive Pacifism

Peace is not merely the absence of war; that is at best negative
peace, a condition necessary but insufficient for a more genuine and
complete positive peace. Pacifism goes well beyond moral opposition to war and involves commitment to order arising from within
society by the cooperative participation of its members. This is to
be contrasted with the sort of order found in societies orderly due
to imposed domination from outside themselves.

Identifying and fostering the conditions that build and sustain
cooperative internal social order is making positive peace. Many
people are devoted to this work to varying degrees, but often they
work from within a warist bias. That is, while trying to build cooperative internal social order by working for justice, many people
share a conceptual outlook shaped by taking war for granted. War
is simply what nations do; lawbreakers—individuals, groups, or
nations breaking civil statutes, social mores, or international agreements—are dealt with violently.

The warist perspective distorts positive peace work not only by
separating means and ends from one another but also by endorsing
means incompatible with desired ends. Cooperative internal social
order cannot be imposed by force from outside, not just because of
practical difficulties but because such means contradict the very ends
sought. Warism distorts the work of positive peace by making it

punitive, defensive, protectionist, and status quo fixated. The result diminishes and undermines positive peace and reinforces the warist outlook in a self-fulfilling way. Within a warist context, positive peace becomes an ideal taken for granted by and for those with power and privilege and those close to them, but often denied to others, especially to distant, different, and otherwise "foreign" others.

When positive peace work is conjoined with moral awareness of warism, universal recognition of human rights and moral opposition to war, that is, when conjoined with critical pacifism, a more genuine and complete notion of positive peace emerges. What is more, such peace is possible because the means employed do not contradict the ends sought.

For pacifists, nonviolence is the appropriate means to peace. Better put, making peace involves the union of ends and means so that peace is not an isolated objective but a policy we live out. As Gandhi sees it, we obtain the exact results of the means we adopt:

> If I want to deprive you of your watch, I shall certainly have to fight for it; if I want to buy your watch, I shall have to pay for it; and if I want a gift, I shall have to plead for it; and, according to the means I employ, the watch is stolen property, my own property, or a donation.[7]

Clearly, different means entail different results. Since pacifists resist means incompatible with desired ends, nonviolent direct action becomes the focus of positive peace.

Contrary to popular opinion, positive peace is a common phenomenon, so common we hardly notice it. As Mulford Sibley notes,

> whenever channels of discussion remain open; parliamentary bodies genuinely deliberate; courts adjudicate under specified rules of law; citizens are consulted about the formation of public policy; the police use physical force if at all only in a discriminating and non-injurious way; and problems of social justice occupy a central place in political discussion—wherever conditions of this kind obtain, fundamentals of nonviolence, both as means and as ends, already exist. Naturally, the exponent of nonviolence will seek to sustain and expand such patterns.[8]

Peacemaking is getting along in orderly ways without that order being imposed by others from outside. Often it rests on mutual agreements understood in context. The test of our peacemaking is how we resolve conflicts as they arise; rarely is our first inclination to use violence.

An exhaustive delineation of nonviolent direct-action techniques cannot be included here. But a broad description, especially of techniques used in conflict resolution, will be helpful. Perhaps the first choice of peaceful means to resolve conflict is discussion leading to consensus. This requires full and equal participation of conflicting parties and depends on mutual respect and recognition of one another's legitimate claims, plus willingness to listen, to be open and honest. It also involves genuine good will on the part of participants, a willingness to work for mutual advantage rather than narrow self-interest.

Where consensus cannot be achieved, negotiation and even arbitration may be used. Always mutual respect and recognition of the other's perspective is needed, as well as willingness to abide by the adjudicator's decision. Negotiation and arbitration can be informal as well as formal. They may involve explicit procedures of legal systems; policies of organizations, schools or businesses; or rest on merely implicit understandings of individuals in conflict who have failed at consensus through discussion but who are committed, even subconsciously, to peaceful resolution of differences.

Failing resolution by negotiation or adjudication, an aggrieved party or group committed to nonviolence might undertake protest including demonstration, petitioning, lobbying, picketing, letter-writing campaigns, marches, teach-ins, and the like. Further down the road toward physical confrontation are methods of noncooperation such as social and economic boycotts, slowdowns, strikes, tax protests, walkouts, economic embargoes, and so on.

Beyond noncooperation is nonviolent intervention. Fasting, sit-ins, and various acts of civil disobedience all short of violent intervention may be attempted. Pacifists may fall anywhere along the range of nonviolent direct-action techniques. Their attempt is always to secure peace through recognizing and building upon the internal character of peaceful order. Pacifists emphasize convictions, their own as well as the convictions of those with whom they are in conflict.

Nonviolent direct-action techniques vary with the degree of coerciveness they carry. True consensus involves genuine mutual agreement; no one is coerced. Negotiation requires a bit more give-and-take, choices are more constrained, and so on down the line, coercion increasing by degree. By the other end of the nonviolent direct-action spectrum, coercion is a more predominant feature of techniques, yet still stopping short of physical violence.

Pacifists vary over the degree of coercion they will employ or endorse. War is extreme violence; it employs coercion in the extreme. Violence is extreme force; if it is less coercive than war it is only due to differences in scale. Pacifists morally reject war; rarely sanction violence; try to reduce if not completely avoid coercion; and generally minimize force in creating personal, social, and international order. Again, different pacifists fall in different places along this continuum. Wherever they fall, nonviolence is easier said than done, given the predominant warist context.

In its primary use, "violence" refers to swift, extreme physical force typically involving injury and violation to persons or property. Hannah Arendt thinks it is its swiftness and extreme forcefulness that attracts us to violence.[9] One party to a conflict feels wronged, angry—even enraged—and feels a need to do something to set matters right immediately. Doing nothing seems somehow untenable even if employing extreme physical force risking injury and violation is not likely to help matters.

There is increasing philosophical interest in a wider use of the term extending beyond the overtly physical domain to covert, psychological and institutional violence.[10] In this broader sense of the term, racism, sexism, economic exploitation including developmentalism, ethnic and religious persecution, homophobia, naturism and even warism are examples of violence. They all involve constraints that injure and violate; they all have entrapping, coercive effects. Pacifists—literally peacemakers—tend to work toward the abolition of these various dominating "isms" as a natural feature of their commitment to positive peace.[11]

The extended notion of violence in covert, psychological, or institutional forms as contrasted with overt, physical forms, adds further complications to understanding and working toward positive peace. Can violence in its extended or even in just its primary forms be avoided completely? The question overwhelms even the most extreme pacifists. Whatever the ultimate answer, pacifists are committed to living lives that minimize violence, coercion, and force, making choices for less rather than more violence even if they cannot achieve pure nonviolence. While often defending the efficacy of pacifist choices as leading to the peaceful results desired more often than do warist choices, many pacifists see pacifism as a virtue to develop and embrace. A moral life is as much a matter of character as of results.

Peace and the Status Quo

The status quo may be the greatest obstacle to expanding the ranks of pacifists. This is because the conventional understanding of

"keeping the peace" is "preserving and protecting the status quo."
Any threat to the way things are, whether in the form of military
or ideological enemies from the outside or revolutionary forces
within, and even mere criticism, progressive reform, and calls for
change from inside or out, all provoke defensive posturing and prep-
arations designed to maintain and preserve existing arrangements.

Most of those who understand keeping the peace to be maintaining the status quo enjoy an advantageous position within it. That
is, they are relatively well-off in comparison with the social, economic, political, environmental, educational, psychological, cultural, or physical health of their peers, neighbors, near, and especially
distant fellow humans. Anything threatening their relative advantage
seems to warrant "defense against aggression." Rarely do those in
positions of relative advantage take their favored status to be linked
to the relative disadvantage of others, although it may well be so
in many cases. The point here is neither to insist on nor deny the
value of egalitarian distribution of the various goods cited above.
Rather, the point is to understand the prevailing attitude that any
threat to the current conditions somehow "justifies" putting down
such threats, with violence if necessary.

Pacifism challenges such widely held and deeply entrenched assumptions about peace, war, violence, and the status quo. This is
part of the reason that pacifists, despite their small numbers, tend
to be regarded with suspicion by mainstream attitudes.

It is not only those in positions of relative advantage who may
be inclined to link peace with things as they are. People in relative
disadvantage may connect peace with the status quo as well, and,
having made the connection, may reject pacifism since they are not
committed to a peace that preserves their disadvantage. This is why
pacifism is taken to be radical by some and conservative by others.
And those in a middle condition between advantaged and disadvantaged may defend the status quo as something worth preserving
since, after all, they could be worse off and, if they accept the
culture's dominant myth, they may one day be better off. Besides,
change promises the unfamiliar. Unless conditions are really bad,
social inertia favors maintaining things as they are.

Moving from the societal to the international level, existing powers have obvious vested interests in the existing geopolitical pattern. After all, they are powers within the structure, and heads of
state do not want national stature to be diminished during their
terms. It is possible that change could work to their advantage,
yet for all but the weakest nations, the unknowns and potential

instability of change provoke concern that it may reduce their relative advantage. The safe course is to avoid risk and defend the status quo. Parallel to the social considerations of individuals raised above, nations are inclined to identify peace with the existing patterns, current boundaries, and known arrangements, however accidental, unjust, or even arbitrary such arrangements might be. All of this is complicated by diverse histories, animosities, alliances, uneven distribution of natural resources, multinational corporate interests, ethnic and religious differences, previous colonization, geopolitical spheres of influence, available labor pools, trade balance and imbalance, and so on. Such considerations result in inordinate amounts of time, energy, and resources being invested in preserving the status quo.

Within this international context it is not surprising that the greatest economic and military powers have tended to use their relative advantage in efforts to expand and certainly preserve those very advantages. Despite a constant flow of peace rhetoric from their leaders, great powers tend to spread weapons throughout the world largely in efforts to secure their own status. This makes perfect sense within the context of identifying peace as the status quo. Negative peace is the goal; justice is not allowing challenges to the existing arrangement. When peace is understood in a positive way, as internal order based on agreement, the applicable understanding of justice is much broader, requiring respect for human rights, freedom from exploitation, full participation in government, etc. For genuine positive peace to flourish, order must arise from within by agreement rather than rest on domination—economic or military—from the outside. For societies to be orderly from within by agreement, justice must be prevalent. And for nations to be orderly with one another by mutual agreement rather than by domination or threat from outside, international justice must prevail.

The Context of Intervention

Having reviewed dominant warist values and having considered a variety of critical as well as positive pacifist views, we can now begin reflecting on humanitarian intervention itself. The context for such reflections must be the current geopolitical situation and the current prevailing values.

Given geopolitical realities, intervention is seen and morally appraised most often from dominant—that is, warist—values. Much of the dominant-culture discussion focuses on arguing for the right to employ military intervention. War realists and just-warists have fundamentally different takes on intervention. Whereas the just-warist is guided by the just-war tradition in determining the moral acceptability of intervention in a given case, war realists are not.

War realism sees war and morality as separate realms. Morality and war simply do not mix. For the war realist, morality inappropriately restrains war when the focus needs to be on winning wars as quickly and efficiently as possible. Morality happens between people within societies and cultures; but war happens between nations, and nations are not within societies or cultures. Nations may be allied with other nations in mutual defense agreements and so on, but the fundamental obligation of a nation is defending and advancing itself and its interests, according to war realists. Nations are neither moral nor immoral; nations are amoral, outside of morality.

The *Realpolitik* of the cold war functions along the war-realist vision. Political realists are those unburdened by morality and sentiment, thereby free to accept the "real world" for the power struggle that they take it to be. Power, we are told, is the name of the game because it is the only thing our enemies understand. Robert Holmes reminds us that "political realism has been the most influential outlook on international affairs in twentieth-century American thought" including such influential proponents as Reinhold Niebuhr, George Kennan, Arthur Schlesinger, Jr. and Henry Kissinger.[12] All see "peace from strength" as the only viable international military policy, echoing George Washington's comment from his first address to both houses of Congress: "to be prepared for war is one of the most effectual means of preserving peace." The strength war realists have in mind in their peace from strength policy is the ability to dominate, to force, to coerce, to get their way. Such strength manifests itself in various ways. It may be military, economic or political, and it may be more or less overt. A nation may invade and overwhelm militarily, it may threaten invasion, or it may use veiled threats to get what it wants. Political and economic involvements also admit of degree. They may involve explicit colonization, neocolonial exploitation, a more subtle drain of the wealth of labor or resources under the guise of "developmental aid," and so on. For realists, none of these forms of involvement in nations outside their own require moral consideration.

The consequences of political realism for international affairs and especially for wars of intervention are fairly straightforward. Only the naive and unrealistic bring moral considerations to bear on issues of conflict among nations. "Hard realities" require constant preparation for and threat of war to protect and advance national interests. According to realists, only the weak and sentimental raise moral concerns and they are dismissed as well-meaning but foolish, or even dangerous, because such misguided moralizing can undermine the effectiveness of a nation's military capacity, political credibility, and economic interests.

The contrast between war realism and just-warism is glaring on one point: just-warists embrace the relevance of morality to war, both concerning going to war and concerning conduct in war, whereas war realists reject moral considerations as irrelevant on both counts. For war realists, only protecting and extending national interests through strength are relevant.

Here we should note a paradox facing war realists that complicates the context of intervention. Although realism itself regards morality to be irrelevant to the conduct of foreign policy, political realities necessitate appropriation of the language of the just-war tradition to win popular support for adventurist military policies. This further complicates making sense of national policy and official judgments regarding morality and war, and it provides evidence for Michael Walzer's observation that "one of the things most of us want, even in war, is to act or to seem to act morally."[13]

One consequence of the appropriation of just-war traditional language by war realists is an emphasis on the "just-cause" provisions while simultaneously ignoring the other *jus ad bellum* conditions as well as the moral restraint guidelines for engagement provided within *jus in bello* rules. The just-war tradition gets perverted not by its authentic proponents but by war realists using the tradition's language to win a needed political following. This leads to a fast and loose employment of just-war moral guidelines and has undermined popular understanding of the tradition. Genuine just-war moralists find themselves caught in an increasingly war-realist context within which the discussion takes place.

The result for pacifists of this twentieth-century drift toward increasingly war-realist international policy has been marginalization to near invisibility. Pacifists are caricatured as mystic moral fanatics and dismissed on the strength of that false image. Pacifist perspectives rarely get taken seriously because "everybody knows" how blatantly silly pacifism is. Again the dominant warist context smothers consideration of a full range of options because thinking about morality, international conflict, peace, and war is structured by a conceptual scheme that itself is biased against moral restraint and nonviolence.

Recognizing warist presumptions and being aware of nonviolent alternatives, pacifists challenge dominant judgments in efforts to provoke rethinking of assumptions, values, and beliefs. In broad terms there are two lines of pacifist objection to aggressively interventionist foreign policy. First, critical pacifists of various sorts question interventions by objecting to and challenging the alleged justifications offered by war realists and just-warists. This may be thought of as the critical or negative side of pacifist perspectives on intervention. Second, positive pacifists of various sorts challenge interventions by objecting to the virtual neglect of nonviolent direct action alternatives to the violence employed.

It should be clear that pacifist perspectives on intervention are as many, rich, and varied—or more so—as are the types of pacifism described above. What follows certainly is not and cannot be an exhaustive treatment either of pacifist perspectives nor of cases of intervention. Rather, it is a philosophical consideration of various pacifist challenges to intervention including mention of specific interventions and of cases where interventions were not undertaken. The challenges flow from pacifist values and the interventions cited, all post-World War II cases, are mentioned only to illuminate the philosophical principles through which pacifist perspectives emerge. This treatment keeps the focus on the logic and implications of various value principles and makes no attempt to offer detailed social and political histories of specific cases.

Pacifist Critiques of Intervention

The most prominent of pacifist objections to various interventions made in the post-World War II international arena focuses on the just-cause provision of the just-war tradition. Nations claim the right to intervene within the borders of other nations to aid secessionists in fostering "national liberation," to counter interventions of other outside nations, or to protect victims of egregious human rights violations like genocide, enslavement, massacre, and so on.[14] Two sorts of pacifist objections frequently get raised. One emphasizes the selectivity, inconsistency, even capriciousness, of applying such grounds for intervention. The other emphasizes the neglect of the other five conditions of *jus ad bellum*. Even if the just-cause condition is met, it alone cannot justify intervention.

Concerning the selectivity with which interventions are justified on the basis of the just-cause provision, a few examples should suffice to illustrate. A US-led international effort insisted that Iraq had to be driven out of Kuwait immediately upon committing blatant aggression in 1990; yet Israel has been allowed to invade and hold lands of neighboring Egypt, Jordan, Lebanon, and Syria dating to the 1967 war in some cases. In the former Yugoslavia, "ethnic cleansing" during the early 1990s has brought thousands of deaths and created hundreds of thousands of refugees while great powers have not intervened except with token United Nations' famine relief and medical aid. Pol Pot's 1975-78 Cambodian reign brought death to hundreds of thousands—some say as many as three million—through execution, starvation and overwork, again without outside intervention. The United States intervened in Panama in the late 1980s to arrest Manuel Noriega for drug trafficking but did not intervene in El Salvador to end death-squad activity or in China to support the pro-democracy movement. Intervention in Somalia in 1992 was supposed to restore order and aid humanitarian efforts to distribute food to starving masses, but intervention has not been used in most cases of widespread starvation. These comments are not to defend or reject any particular intervention. The point is to illustrate that powers act on their right to intervene very selectively. When like cases are treated differently, pacifists suspect motives for intervention to be other than the noble causes cited. This is where the just-war tradition is especially vulnerable to appropriation and abuse by war realists. Narrow self-interest—access to cheap oil, promoting strategic advantage, exploiting markets or cheap labor abroad, exploiting opinion polls at home, and so on—gets disguised with moral language to counter objections to blatant and cynical political realism.

The virtual neglect of the other five *jus ad bellum* conditions— and with that neglect the suggestion that a just cause warrants any and all necessary means—constitutes a more complicated set of pacifist objections to intervention. Looking at each condition separately exposes some of the complexity.

Even among proponents of the just-war tradition, opinions differ on who constitutes right authority. In the United States, executive and legislative branches of government periodically debate the issue, with Congress and the president each claiming authority. In the case of the Persian Gulf War, the Bush administration built a United Nations-based international coalition in advance of the congressional vote making the latter a mere formality, a vote of confidence for what was a done deal. In the fall 1994 intervention in Haiti, the Jimmy Carter and Colin Powell eleventh-hour negotiations with Raoul Cedras, aided by reports of a U.S. invasion force having taken off for Haiti even as the discussions were under way, substituted occupation for invasion, thus precluding much of the congressional will to challenge the Clinton administration policy. There is much disagreement over who counts as right authority: a given head of state, a given nation's legislative body, the collective will of United Nations members, the UN Secretary General or Security Council, speakers for major religious groups, and so on. As with other aspects of the just-war tradition, this is no simple matter.

Right intention may be even more problematic. According to the tradition, the only right intention in just war is to bring about peace. Intending revenge, domination, harm, or cruelty is always wrong. And intention is always wrong if personal, ethnic, religious, or national self-interest is paramount. Where available evidence suggests mixed motives at best, assurance that any particular intervention follows right intention is very difficult to secure, especially when other candidates for intervention are neglected. Occasional Bosnians have suggested—not entirely facetiously—that they might have received military help from the West had Bosnia been an oil-rich country.

The fourth condition that must be satisfied to justify going to war is that war must be undertaken only as a last resort. All avenues for righting the wrong that prompted the just-cause decision must be exhausted prior to military action. The just-war tradition is built on the presumption that war is abhorrent and must be avoided if at all possible. The increasing influence of war realism and the sheer speed of events brought on by modern technology have resulted in downplaying this provision, especially where important national interests are at stake. Nations often rush to employ military means despite the moral restraint rule that prohibits military action unless it is a last resort. On the other hand, where national self-interest is less pressing, nations often invoke moral restraint rhetoric and project a peace image. Pacifists object to the self-serving convenience and inconsistency with which this provision is administered.

Further, the prevailing warism precludes considering less violent and nonviolent alternatives to military means. Rarely can even the most genuine just-warist insist that every alternative to violent intervention was exhausted prior to a given military action. Regarding the Gulf War, economic sanctions were given only months before being declared ineffective, hardly exhausting alternatives to war. In South Africa, sanctions were in place for years before their effects were factors in negotiations to dismantle apartheid. Vested interests may be factors in explaining patience in one case and rush to war in the other. Economic interests prevailed over humanitarian concerns when China's "most-favored-nation" trade status was extended despite lack of progress on respect for human rights, especially of dissidents. The US bombing raid on Libya's Moamar Khadafy during the Reagan administration appeared to be more a first than a last resort. Yet just-war rhetoric was brought out to excuse the surprise attack. Clearly administration of the last-resort provision varies widely. It seems to be manipulated at the convenience of decision makers, used to excuse or rationalize acts more likely designed to preserve the status quo. Enemies get humanized or demonized depending on which appropriation of moral language will best influence public opinion to the speaker's advantage.

The just-war tradition also requires that war be undertaken only if it is likely to create conditions fostering a lasting, emergent peace. Such conditions would have to set right the problems that contributed to the failure of the former peace. Where internal, collaborative, and cooperative order breaks down, it is not enough to impose external, dominating force to restore a semblance of order. The tradition requires the creation of conditions likely to sustain internal, cooperative order. After all, dominating occupying forces are not expected to remain in place indefinitely. From the pacifist perspective, this is among the least of concerns to those making decisions about intervention in part because interventions tend to be military and military force is virtually antithetical to internal order. Had the Bush administration considered this provision prior to intervention in Somalia in 1992 it might have saved lives and precluded frustration and suffering.

Hannah Arendt makes an important point in *On Violence* that is relevant here. Arendt is interested in explaining the increasing advocacy of violence in the contemporary world and in challenging Mao Tse-tung's claim that "power grows out of the barrel of a gun." She articulates the position not only that power is not based on violence but, further, that power and violence are opposites. On her view, the extreme of violence is one against all, where the one has access to implements of destruction; the extreme of power is all against one, with power depending upon an agent's capacity to act in concert with others. So, consensus, cooperation, collaboration, and group agreement constitute power, whereas access to implements of great force and destruction constitutes violence. One can be violent on one's own if one has the necessary implements. One can be powerful only in the company of and with the cooperation of others. Loss of power often leads individuals—or nations—to attempt replacing lost power with violence. But violence is the opposite of power and cannot stand in its stead.[15]

Given Arendt's point on the relationship of violence to power, pacifists note that military actions can force order by external domination (that is, they can exercise violence) but they cannot create internal order by cooperation (that is, they cannot generate power). The internal order that constitutes positive peace arises from power, the opposite of military violence, which may impose only negative peace. Perhaps this fundamental incongruity between military action and lasting peace accounts for the typical neglect of the emergent-peace provision.

The last *jus ad bellum* condition is the principle of proportionality. According to this requirement, war may be justly undertaken only if the total good likely to come from the war outweighs the total evil of making it. A war is disproportionate and thus cannot be just when the price of a projected intervention is too great in total dislocation, suffering, and death for all involved—not just for the intervening power. Figuring costs must include direct as well as indirect human, economic, cultural, historic, and environmental factors, by comparison with the good likely to come from it, again considering all likely gains. Pacifists suspect that projections of gains and losses tend to fall wide of realities. Those caught in a warist mindset tend to exaggerate their own strengths and the enemy's evils while underestimating likely losses and risks, in part because they are incapable of considering alternatives. As Nietzsche is reputed to have put it, if the only tool you have is a hammer, everything begins to look like a nail.

Considering pacifist objections based on the various *jus ad bellum* provisions of the just-war tradition only begins a look at pacifist critiques of intervention. After all, even if all six of the requirements for justly going to war were met, still there are objections to how various interventions are conducted. Again, examples are meant only to illustrate pacifist objections. This is not meant to be an exhaustive consideration of any of the interventions mentioned.

The *jus in bello* moral guidelines for conduct in war set requirements for moral restraint to limit the evils caused by war. The fundamental restraining condition is that it is always wrong to cause injury, suffering, death, destruction, or dislocation to innocents. Participants in just war must act to discriminate between legitimate and illegitimate targets for all acts of war. It is never permissible to target innocents, although their injury, suffering, or death may be excused if they were unintended victims. Pacifists toward the absolutist end of the spectrum tend to object to the double-effect clause that acknowledges harm to innocents as wrong but excuses it as unavoidable, unintended, collateral loss. Their objection is to a moral guideline that excuses evil through a very fine and difficult if not impossible distinction. They wonder, for example, how one can morally maintain a notion of suffering that is foreseen but unintended, so that a bombing raid can go forward against a military target knowing that innocent bystanders will be lost. If the bombing is intentional and its collateral effects predictable, and if persons it would be wrong to target are foreseeable victims of the bombing, then by what moral principle can one excuse the act? Somehow it seems less than satisfactory to separate intended, appropriate targets from unintended, inappropriate ones when all are foreseeable victims.

Pacifists from nearer the pragmatic end of the continuum may concede the distinction in principle but object that it is outrageously abused in fact. Some objectors to various military actions during the Persian Gulf War condemn the war not for lack of a just cause or any other *jus ad bellum* condition but simply because various actions abandoned moral restraint and took little care to avoid harm to innocents. Ramsey Clark documents over 109,000 aerial sorties over Iraq dropping 88,500 tons of explosives in a forty-two day assault on Iraqi infrastructure beginning January 17, 1991. He notes that frequent military claims to high accuracy for the U.S. bombing effort during the war only underscore the fact that schools, hospitals, homes, water treatment facilities, food distribution centers, and so on were targeted, since they were destroyed by such precise means. But it is a crime of war to have such targets. Trying to have it both ways, officials always dismissed such losses as collateral damage.[16]

Even conceding rather implausibly extended applications of the principle of double effect still leaves US Persian Gulf War practices open to the charge of disproportionality, since it is highly questionable whether the alleged good to have been gained by such wanton destruction was achieved. Even if it was, it is not clear that such gains outweigh in good the evils employed to secure the achievement.

On the basis of reviewing the moral-restraint guidelines of the just-war tradition alone pacifists find ample grounds to question most interventions. Pacifists from differing points along the pacifist continuum will base their objections on varying grounds reflecting their respective pacifist views. But pacifist criticisms of intervention are not limited to objections to the application of just-war guidelines. Genuine just-warists might well share many of the objections sketched above.

Critical pacifist objections to intervention need not rest on exposing inconsistent, uneven, or hypocritical application of just-war moral-restraint guidelines. They may flow directly from particular pacifist positions as well. Certainly absolute pacifists object to every military intervention as instances of their general rejection of force. Collectivist pacifists base their critique of intervention on their moral principle allowing only small-scale, interpersonal, protective violence, never allowing force on the scale of troops invading nations. Fallibility pacifists may concede the just-war principles in theory but question the sufficiency of knowledge warranting mass violence while proponents of various sorts of technological pacifism point out the likely spillage of violence and harm brought on by modern means of war and argue that the harm to people, other life forms, and earth itself outweighs the good likely to be gained. Pragmatic pacifists may underscore the factual history of war's failures as well as question the wisdom of believing various military means are likely to solve the problems provoking thoughts of intervention. And they may do so in general or on a case-by-case basis.

Moving to the positive as distinct from the negative pacifist perspectives, pacifists holding widely divergent views generally agree that the primary moral problem with most so-called humanitarian interventions is that the means of intervention employed undercut the moral integrity of the intervention. That is, pacifists often believe that egregious human rights violations do in fact warrant intervention. As was mentioned above, very few pacifists are passivists, wishing to do nothing in the face of evil. The problem is in making sure intervention is the best course and in finding ways to make interventions genuinely humanitarian.

Pacifists object to using allegations of moral wrong as excuses for violence, especially when nonviolent alternatives get ignored or dismissed. Pacifists are not opposed to intervention per se. But they are cautious, wary, suspicious of intervention, because genuine peace must be built from within. The best possible result of imposition from the outside is merely negative peace, and even it is achieved at great human cost and rarely lasts. Western cultures have been slow to learn to resist the temptation to intervene for the purpose of "fixing" problem situations. In most cases of military intervention, the actions undertaken make matters worse. Where intervention is warranted, pacifists seek methods of nonviolent and thus more genuinely humanitarian intervention. This is the pacifist commitment to positive peace, something mass violence can never create.

Nonviolent Intervention

The positive side of pacifism is perhaps both most important and least considered when it comes to moral evaluations of intervention. Most such discussions focus on debates over when to permit violence. Warist bias tends to preclude consideration of nonviolent intervention. Pacifism is simply dismissed as unrealistic; "everybody knows" nonviolence doesn't work. The warist context within which interventions are considered settles the issue before it is raised.

While conventional wisdom suggests that nonviolence doesn't work, pacifists are inclined to insist that, indeed, nonviolence is the only thing that has ever worked and that will ever work if we think seriously about what *working* means. For pacifists, the goal is positive peace; social and political order arising from within groups by cooperation. A policy or technique works if it creates and sustains such conditions. Warists, on the other hand, are inclined to understand peace as status quo social and political arrangements in the absence of war. They are caught in a negative conception of peace. So, to preserve things as they are from various threats, warists construct elaborate justifications for imposing order onto groups from the outside by military domination. Such means work to some extent at preserving the status quo, but they don't work at creating positive peace. This is what pacifists have in mind when insisting that nonviolence is the only thing that can work. Violence is antithetical to the desired objective of internal, cooperative, sustainable social and political order.

The varying degrees of nonviolent direct-action techniques raised above suggest types of nonviolent intervention to consider. Of course cooperative discussion and negotiation are least coercive and thus first used. When they fail to resolve the moral grounds provoking intervention, third-party-assisted arbitration may work. This may be formal as in the case of World Court hearings, or it may be informal, where a disengaged nation trusted by both conflicting nations acts as arbitrator. Like discussion and negotiation, arbitration only works to the extent that conflicting nations are committed to abiding by arbitration decisions. The value of arbitration is seriously undermined when major powers go to arbitration, lose decisions, and refuse to abide by those decisions. The Reagan administration dismissal of the World Court's opinion on the US blockade of Nicaragua in 1986 is a case in point. Major powers lead by example. Trumpeting the importance of international principles and bodies when they serve a nation's narrow interests yet ignoring or dismissing them when they do not exposes that nation's hypocrisy and undermines the process of positive peace at the same time.

Where arbitration fails, various forms of noncooperation may come into play. Cultural and economic boycotts as well as withholding aid, freezing assets, and imposing various other economic and political sanctions may be considered. This is an important yet very complicated set of issues not to be treated lightly. Economic sanctions, for example, may require years to take effect, and the evil warranting intervention may be too immediate to allow waiting for long-term pressure to generate results. Or the sanctions may affect innocents rather than those responsible for the horrors demanding attention and thus nonviolence could compound rather than solve problems. There are a host of subtle and complex contingencies to take into consideration and always there are a great many unknowns. All of this is complicated further by the pacifist wish to minimize coercion of any kind, to avoid covert as well as overt forms of violence.

Nonviolence is not a quick fix. But, then, neither is violence. While conventional wisdom presumes the justifiability of violent intervention and dismisses nonviolence as unrealistic, we must recognize that violence does not work all of the time even to create negative peace. And as argued above, violence cannot give us what we really want. Only nonviolence can in principle create the genuine positive peace desired. So, for all its shortcomings, nonviolence may be essential to genuine resolution of the problems provoking intervention. And whatever else may be said in weighing violent against nonviolent options, we know violent intervention will bring injury, destruction, and suffering even on the occasions when it is said to have worked to achieve its goals. And when violence fails, nothing redeems the evil of the means. Nonviolence, on the other hand, minimizes coercion and force making its successes uncompromised. Its failures fall short of the positive peace desired but at least they do not add to the suffering and destruction as do violent "successes" and failures.

Perhaps the least-explored options of nonviolent direct action go beyond the noncooperation of sanctions to actual intervention in the form of nonviolent invasion. Witness for Peace actions in Central America in the 1980s and 1990s have brought hundreds of nonviolent direct-action volunteers to put themselves between hostile groups or to amass themselves in territory in order to protect it and its inhabitants from military invasion and shelling. The nonviolent activists are human shields, unarmed and unwilling to fight aggressively yet standing in solidarity with victims of aggression, calling for international attention to expose and end the human rights abuses.

Most widely publicized nonviolent human-shield actions have been undertaken by unarmed locals standing against violent intervention. The Hands Across the Baltics actions in Latvia, Estonia and Lithuania in 1990 were actions to deter Soviet occupation as the Baltic republics defended their independent sovereignty. The human barricades of women, children and old men in Chechnya held off tanks and briefly deterred Russian invaders in late 1994. While such actions are not interventionist but defensive, organized internally and designed to protect nations from violent intervention, Witness for Peace actions use the same nonviolent direct-action techniques to create a form of nonviolent invasion. Nonviolent direct activists from outside nations stand in solidarity with victims of violent oppression to provide a buffer to aggression as well as call attention to moral horror, forcing international judgment.

Conventional wisdom tends to regard nonviolent intervention as a largely ineffective step designed only to signal seriousness in the buildup toward violent intervention. In fact nonviolent interventions in the form of economic and political sanctions have been highly effective in bringing about genuine change to reduce oppression. Although conservatives lobbied for years to have widespread international sanctions against the apartheid policies of the government of South Africa discontinued, claiming they were ineffective and actually hurting the people they were designed to help, in fact international sanctions against the Republic of South Africa played a major role in pressing the minority government into negotiations to plan for dismantling apartheid.[17] Potential economic losses to investors present a significant obstacle in the way of greater use of sanctions in support of international human rights. The 1994 U.S. decision extending most-favored-nation trade status to China despite continued human rights abuses has been a setback for genuinely nonviolent efforts to alter the internal human rights practices of China and many other nations as well. Sanctions tend to take months or even years to be effective, and multinational corporations strongly resist policies that block them from markets, natural resources, and sources of inexpensive labor.

Another complicating factor in any consideration of nonviolent intervention is the dominant cultural inclination to misunderstand the concept of violence. Because quiet, covert forms of institutional violence—racism, sexism, homophobia, naturism, and economic exploitation—need not require overt physical force, they are often thought to be nonviolent. And because demonstrations, boycotts, economic sanctions, and nonviolent direct actions sometimes attract violent reactions from dominant institutions, they are often decried as violent themselves. But a crucial difference has been neglected when these concepts are conflated: quiet, covert forms of institutional violence involve defending and extending privileges to an advantaged group through the systematic violation of another group. This is why racism, sexism, and similar institutionalized means of domination are forms of violence. Demonstrations, boycotts, economic sanctions and nonviolent direct actions are genuinely nonviolent when undertaken in solidarity with an exploited, oppressed, or disadvantaged group and when they challenge privileges dependent on such violation.

It is difficult for beneficiaries of systems that advantage some at the expense of others to recognize the unfairness from perspectives within those very systems. This is why those judging from the dominant perspective so often identify peace with the status quo and confuse violence and nonviolence.

One result of such confusion is that allegedly nonviolent development by major power multinational corporations or by government agencies themselves may in fact involve institutional violence. For example, since World War II El Salvador has experienced shrinking traditional agricultural production while export agricultural production has been growing. This trend has been accompanied by an increasing percentage of the population becoming landless. Wealth, created by indigenous labor and resources, has increasingly moved from peasants to capital held by a few very wealthy individuals. The resulting poverty, displacement, and suffering to the working class provoked uprisings that have been put down by a military that had been expanded, equipped, trained, and funded by the outside major power providing the markets for exported agricultural produce. The current situation in Chiapas, Mexico, is essentially a variant of this same process. Privilege, power, exploitation, institutional violence, relative advantage, and defense of the status quo all complicate understanding—and making moral judgments about—any given intervention.

Despite the incredible subtlety and complexity of any particular situation calling for possible intervention, the pacifist point regarding intervention is that genuine, positive peace requires internal, cooperative, sustainable order. Interventions can help only to the extent that they contribute to creating and maintaining such internal order. Interventions that dominate from the outside or prop up exploitation from within cannot achieve positive peace. When critics of nonviolence complain that it does not work, they need to review the historical record, which shows a persistent failure of military intervention at achieving genuine and lasting peace. And they need to reflect on the conditions that create and sustain positive peace. Not only does nonviolence work; it is the only thing that can work.

Moral Horror

After various critical as well as positive pacifist perspectives on humanitarian intervention have been considered, still there remains

a nagging dominant-culture objection that while all of these pacifist notions sound wonderful in theory, they are simply out of phase
with the grisly realities of the real world. What has been said thus
far may cast pacifist reflections in a more favorable light than popular stereotypes would allow, yet the pressing immediacy of what
may be called "moral horror" seems untouched.

"Moral horror" is used here to refer to acts so heinous that they
provoke a visceral response, an ethical shudder perhaps best described as moral outrage. Blatant inhumanities like torture, massacre, death camps, genocide, enslavement, deliberate inflicting of
suffering, and any other acts of cruelty and wanton disregard for
human well-being all qualify as acts provoking moral horror. We
can imagine situations so obviously and grossly in violation of persons that even pacifists may concede violence to be warranted. Such
possibilities need not be merely imagined; the daily news confronts
us with "ethnic cleansing," police brutality, needless starvation, torture, abuse of children, armed aggression, and so on.

As noted above, very few if any pacifists are of the absolute
sort, and even those few who are tend to be so in their aspirations
more than in their actions. So, most pacifists concede the justifiability of some degree of violence in principle. But rarely are pacifists sympathetic with violence in fact, and when they are it is
toward small-scale, interpersonal uses of protective force rather than
mass violence, large-scale and aggressive. But if most pacifists do
not find themselves sympathetic with war or military intervention
to the point of warranting it, are they closet absolute pacifists after
all? Or might they one day be confronted with situations sufficiently horrible that they would warrant war?

Understanding pacifism as a range of views differing from one
another by degree of moral restraint required and by degree of coercion allowed makes pacifism more plausible but it also presents
a dilemma to nonabsolute pacifists. If one accepts any violence at
all, then how is the line drawn among degrees of violence? What
guides the distinction between allowable and forbidden violence?

One approach to this question is to consider the context in which
violence tends to erupt. As noted above, most of us take peace for
granted most of the time. Rarely does it even occur to us that it is
peace we are making. We simply presume a measure of goodwill,
mutual respect, and shared desire for cooperative order. The problem arises when the peace is broken, especially when peacebreak-
ers threaten, exploit, or attack existing goodwill, mutuality, and

cooperative order. When self-imposed orderliness of internal agreement, cooperation and collaboration breaks down under attack from
the outside, then the temptations to justify and employ violence
grow.

Many reflecting on this issue may well think the reasons for the
turn to violence are obvious: we persist in peacemaking only so long
as the internal agreement, cooperation, collaboration, and mutuality
work; when they fail to work—as in cases involving moral horror—
we try to impose order from the outside, using violent means, willing to settle for negative peace as a lesser of evils. But this appeal
to what works is too simple. After all, warmakers do not give up
on war when it fails; rather, they alter specific acts of war, trying
new strategies or new tactics, or they go down in defeat without
giving up their violent means. Furthermore, exemplary peacemakers—e.g., Mohandas Gandhi, Jane Addams, Albert Schweitzer, Dor-
othy Day, Martin Luther King, Jr. and Nelson Mandela[18]—do not
give up on nonviolence when it fails to secure their desired goals.
In fact, exemplary peacemakers are known as such in large part
because of their persistence in nonviolence even in the face of defeat. So, failure alone does not account for the ease with which
nonviolence is often abandoned.

Part of the problem is that despite the common habits of peace,
we are nurtured in the values of violence. The warist predispositions discussed above embrace violence as an unfortunate but necessary and justifiable means to defend and secure ourselves, our kin,
our property, and selected others with whom we share interests or
agreements. The dominant presumption is that we may take up violent means whenever the stakes are high and nonviolence seems
unlikely to guarantee success. So, while our habits may be peaceful, violence is the accepted alternative for exceptional circumstances, and we allow plenty of situations to be considered
exceptional. Violent intervention needs no special justification since
it is widely regarded as quite ordinary and legitimate.

Clearly, the broad cultural acceptability of violence and war itself needs explaining. How is it that while most of us most of the
time have the habits of peace, still most of us accept war and violence as reasonable alternatives when peace habits break down?

In *On Violence* Hannah Arendt suggests that the answer is in the
relationship between violence and rage. As she reminds us, it is a
commonplace to realize that very often violence emerges from rage.
Rage may be pathological or irrational—highly publicized cases of

random machine-gunning of ordinary people in public places come to mind—but rage may be perfectly sane and rational also. For Arendt, "only where there is reason to suspect that conditions could be changed and are not does rage arise. Only when our sense of justice is offended do we react with rage. . . ."[19] Outrageous events—the moral horrors of torture, genocide, starvation, concentration camps, death squads, any extreme exploitation or cruelty— tempt us to resort to violence. Arendt thinks it is the "inherent immediacy and swiftness" of violence that accounts for the temptations to use it. "In private as well as in public life there are situations in which the very swiftness of a violent act may be the only remedy."[20] This is why Arendt takes the position that violence may be justifiable yet it can never be legitimate. Legitimacy, for Arendt, rests on agreements and associations in the past, like the establishment of rules for government, whereas justifiability rests on a clear and present opportunity to right the tipped scales of justice immediately. Violence is presumed to be a quick fix, or at least the chance of one. Nonviolence takes time.

The pacifist's dilemma is knowing how to respond to moral horror, knowing when, if ever, violence may be justified and knowing the limits of its justifiability. For absolute pacifists the dilemma does not arise: violence is wrong always, everywhere, for everyone under all possible circumstances. But the dilemma does arise for the vast majority of actual pacifists: if violence is ever justifiable, how does one avoid sliding down the slippery slope to the frequent extension and abuse of such justifiability in principle to find oneself in the current climate, taking violence and war for granted and finding moral reluctance to make war and violence to be naive and in need of justification? That is, how do peacemakers justify taking positions between the extremes of absolute pacifism and the easy rationalization to use violence?

Returning to Arendt we find some help in drawing the line along the spectrum. She says, "no one questions the use of violence in self-defense because the danger is not only clear, but also present, and the end justifying the means is immediate."[21] Setting aside the fact that indeed some pacifists do question violence even in self-defense, Arendt has called attention to important guides to recognizing abuse of the justifiability of violence: the clarity and presence of life-threatening conditions from which we can reasonably expect immediate relief by prompt, violent action. It is precisely such conditions that make plausible using violence to fend off the infamous unprovoked thug in the alley.

Unfortunately, Arendt—and a great many others—have broader and looser standards of clarity, presence, life-threatening conditions, and immediacy of relief than many peacemakers might think warranted. So even with these guidelines to safeguard against the abuse of the justifiability of violence, Arendt allows for greater license in the use of violence and war than would the more exemplary peacemakers cited above. And many allow even greater license than does Arendt. As we saw with just-war principles above, along with conditions to guide and restrain violence comes the risk of abusing such conditions to rationalize violence. One person's moral horror can be another's just deserts.

Recognizing pacifism as a range of views along a moral-restraint continuum complicates drawing any line between justifiable and unacceptable violence. As we have seen, various pacifists draw the line in different places. And proponents of just-war positions do not all draw the line in the same place either. On issues as complex as these we should not be surprised to find a wide range of judgment. Despite broad variation along the moral-restraint continuum, peace advocates persistently work to minimize violence and other forms of coercion, even in the face of moral horror. Although Arendt allows greater license for violence than pacifists condone, still her guidelines may help restrict and reduce violence if they are taken as principles of morality rather than as loopholes to allow violence.

Morally condoning violence only in the face of clear and present life-threatening conditions from which we can reasonably expect to defend ourselves or others by prompt violent action does not put an end to all violence, but taken seriously such convictions can significantly reduce the frequency of justified violence. The conditions outlined are sufficiently restrictive to shrink the scale of warranted violence as well. Proposed acts of mass violence cannot meet the tests of clarity and presence of threats and reasonable expectation for immediate success by prompt action. Small-scale acts of interpersonal violence stand a better chance of satisfying the guidelines, but even they do not get automatic justification. What results is a relationship describing our moral-justification burden: the bigger the scale of proposed violence, the heavier the burden of justification. The use of modern weapons of mass destruction requires exponentially greater justifications due to the scope of such weapons, which is widened because of their indiscriminate destructive capacities. This is because the moral horror of using such weapons approaches or even exceeds that of the evil they are made to be used against. Modern war fails such a justification test.

The reduction in scale of justified violence, prompted by the tests for clarity and presence of threats plus reasonable expectation of immediate success, has the advantage of fitting well with common-sense moral judgments. This helps explain why one need not be a pacifist to feel moral qualms about, say, the firebombing of Dresden or the use of nuclear weapons against Hiroshima and Nagasaki during World War II. And it helps explain why pacifists may oppose war yet feel sympathy with victims of death squads arming themselves with personal weapons to protect their families. Small-scale, clear and present dangers from which we can immediately protect ourselves or close others by swift, contained violent action is much easier for warists to defend and much harder for pacifists to condemn than large-scale, murky, distant danger requiring extended and massive violent action with indiscriminate weapons. Again we are reminded of the scale-reducing analogies used to justify war. They are used because common sense is suspicious of the justifiability of violence, especially on a large scale. The burden of justification for small-scale violence is perhaps possible to bear.

What all this leads to is a recognition that violence may be warranted—depending on one's position along the continuum—in the face of moral horror, especially in small-scale cases of danger where a swift, controlled act of violence seems very likely to set straight the scales of justice immediately. This is why we tend not to hesitate over controlled and restrained uses of force by police officers in the apprehension of criminals. This is also why politicians seeking support for adventurist military interventions speak of invasions as "policing actions."

The U.S. occupation of Haiti begun in the fall of 1994 has been largely acceptable to the American public because it has looked more like police work than like an invasion. It is not actually police work since, by and large, criminals are not being apprehended for trial. But it is not actually an invasion either since the occupation was invited by the elected officials of Haiti and it has not involved mass violence against Haitians or anyone else. Pacifists of various sorts cannot draw an exact line between large-scale police work and small-scale military activities. Sometimes military personnel are called to do large-scale police work domestically as well as internationally—President Eisenhower's use of federal troops to police the integration of schools in Little Rock, Arkansas, in the 1950s is just one case in point. The pacifist test is always whether violence and coercion have been minimized; whether less violence may have been equally or even more successful at attaining the ends in view.

One last thing must be said on the topic of moral horror. The exemplary peacemakers mentioned above all faced moral horror and had every reason to be outraged by the conditions they struggled to change. All of them might have succumbed to the temptation to use, encourage, and support overt violence in the name of justice. Most of the world would have understood and accepted such choices. Certainly Gandhi and King, and more recently Mandela, would have had broad sympathy and support had they called for use of armed means to attain their ends.

The case of Nelson Mandela is especially relevant, given the recent, largely unpredicted, nonviolent revolution in South Africa. The exploitation, abuse, dehumanization, and gross violation of elementary human rights of blacks under the formal policies of apartheid in the Republic of South Africa for nearly half of this century certainly qualify as moral horror. If anyone could earn a right to use arms to achieve justice it would seem the black majority of South Africa had qualified. Within their ranks surely Nelson Mandela would have been particularly justified had he called for armed revolution given his lifetime struggle, including twenty-seven years in prison as a banned person. Mandela himself became notorious in the 1960s for pushing the African National Congress to reconsider its nonviolent policy given the government's commitment to violence in defense of apartheid. He saw nonviolence as a tactic that should be abandoned when it no longer worked, and he could not bear any policy that left ANC activists to be crushed by naked violence.[22] He appealed to the ANC to prepare for the possibility of armed resistance. It is a contemporary miracle that he could persist in leading a nonviolent struggle within such a context. The ongoing, successful, nonviolent revolution in the Republic of South Africa stands as a testimony to nonviolent direct action including discussion, negotiation, arbitration, and nonviolent humanitarian intervention in the form of international sanctions. Mandela's success in building positive peace in South Africa is all the more astounding because it was so unthinkable just a few years ago.

Conclusion

The subject of humanitarian intervention is a complex and difficult one. Pacifist perspectives on humanitarian intervention differ in many ways. Yet there are important general characteristics shared by pacifists of various sorts. Many of the pacifist views emerge through extending and criticizing moral concerns of the just-war tradition, leading to increasing degrees of moral restraint over the use of violence. Pacifists oppose war and other large-scale violence and generally favor reducing domestic and international violence to a bare minimum, expanding the use of nonviolent direct action to build and sustain positive peace. Finally, pacifists tend to favor minimizing coercion, reducing all appeals to force. This involves "a sturdy, public suspicion of organized violence even in the best of causes" (to borrow a phrase from Sara Ruddick).[23] Genuine peace rests on internal order created and maintained through cooperative agreements reached without threat, intimidation, domination, or force from inside or outside groups. Because of this commitment to positive peace, pacifists extend their struggle beyond confronting explicit, overt violence to challenging implicit, covert, or institutional forms of violence like racism, sexism, and homophobia, and oppressions based on class, ethnicity, religion, and the like. Always the means to address grievances and resolve conflicts are chosen with an interest in their compatibility with the ends sought.

Beginning to see justifications for violence as variations of degree along a broad spectrum lends several advantages to the prospects for peace. It opens conversations about reducing violence incrementally, since pacifists and just-warists of various sorts are not moral opposites as popular caricature might suggest. And it thereby depolarizes discussions, recognizing and respecting common moral ground among those with moral concerns regarding violence. This increases the likelihood for positive peace—cooperative and collaborative order based on internal agreement.

Beyond opening less polarized discussions, understanding the range of values on war and peace as commitments to varying degrees of moral restraint and commitments to reduce coercion in its many forms has potential to unite peace-minded individuals in their efforts to back away from war realism, furthering nonviolence and reducing appeals to force. The critical perspectives developed through recognition of the complexity of the range of values on peace and war should lead to raising rather than lowering expectations for justifying violence, with the burden squarely on those who would advocate violence. Attending to the relationship between dominant warist values and the status quo should deepen critical reflections and expand consideration of options beyond warism.

Pacifist perspectives on intervention, when reviewed within the context of our predominant conceptual scheme, begin to appear less deviant and marginal; they begin to reflect better sense than stereotypes would allow. Recognizing positive peace as a commonly accepted and widely maintained set of conditions we enjoy commonly and take for granted for ourselves opens us to entertaining the practicality of nonviolent direct actions more favorably.

Pacifist perspectives cannot immediately solve every situation calling for humanitarian intervention. Pacifists do not have an immediate solution to the horror in Bosnia; but, as should be obvious, neither do warists. Unfortunately, pacifists get asked for their suggestions well after believers in violence have spread weapons and war throughout the region. Very often the asking is an attempt to reduce pacifism to absurdity when war has already shown itself to fail.

The world has labored under the burden of taking violence and war for granted for thousands of years and continues to labor under this unbearable burden. Great powers tend to increase the burden by their assumptions, policies, and the proliferation of weapons, making dangerous people even more dangerous. It is unreasonable to expect this pattern to change overnight by some sort of mass conversion to pacifism. It is still more unreasonable to guarantee that the pattern will not change by claiming that it cannot change at all, insisting that war and violence are natural and inevitable. We got to this point incrementally; if we are to get out of it, it will be little-by-little as well. The few bright signs from Bosnia are not results of military intervention but of internal, cooperative order. They are the glimmers of positive human interaction that happen despite overwhelming conditions to preclude them.

The carnage of the twentieth century demands that something change. We are a sorry species indeed if the best we can do is continue to escalate our threats, multiply our implements of war, and carry out increasingly efficient violence against one another. Violence can satisfy the urge to do something immediate in the face of moral horror, violence can satisfy a desire for revenge against evil, and sometimes violence can impose a short-term negative peace. But violence cannot create and sustain conditions of genuine positive peace because they must come from within by cooperation, which violence cannot create.

Pacifists no more have instant solutions to situations like those in Bosnia or Rwanda than do warists. When conditions deteriorate to the levels of shelling civilians or hacking neighbors with machetes all options are inadequate. The challenge is creating and sustaining conditions where life may flourish, where order is internalized, cooperative, and respectful of human rights rather than conditions of misery where order is imposed, exploitative, domineering, and abusive. The failures in Bosnia and Rwanda are many. If there is any truth to what has been said here, whenever violence erupts it is in anger out of frustration over powerlessness. Our struggle is to foster conditions that preclude or at least reduce powerlessness, that encourage participation, cooperation, and internal initiative sustaining order. For pacifists, nonviolent direct actions can build such conditions while military interventions cannot. For pacifists, the challenge is to make interventions truly humanitarian. This means making them nonviolent.

Converted to practical action such conclusions lead to advancing peacemaking in three ways. First, peacemakers need to expand their critique of the abuse of guidelines for limiting violence. If just-warists would honor even just-war guidelines conscientiously we would at least see a reduction in carnage. Second, peacemakers must encourage narrowing and tightening as opposed to the prevailing culture's broadening and loosening of those value restrictions on violence. That is, peacemakers must press for movement away from warism toward if not into pacifism. And third, peacemakers need to reinforce awareness and encourage expansion of positive peace and its techniques. Not only can positive peace work to reduce violence; it already does, and it is the only thing that ever has.

Notes

I am grateful to Deane Curtin, C. R. Moyer, Karen Warren and Rick Werner for suggestions and reactions to early forms of this essay. I also appreciate the encouragement of colleagues Nancy Holland and Stephen Kellert. Thanks go as well to Hamline University for a Hanna Research Grant for the summer of 1994 and for sabbatical leave from January through August, 1995.

1. I borrow this expression from Deane Curtin. See "Making Peace With the Earth: Indigenous Agriculture and the Green Revolution," *Environmental Ethics* (February, 1995).

2. In describing the conditions of the just-war tradition I broadly follow
Michael Walzer, *Just and Unjust Wars* (New York: Basic Books, 1977) and
James Turner Johnson, *Can Modern Wars Be Just?* (New Haven: Yale Univer-
sity Press, 1984), two widely respected authorities on the subject.

3. Walzer, *Just and Unjust Wars*, 90.

4. The Classical era of Western philosophy is usually taken to be between the seventh century B.C.E. and the fifth century C.E. From the fifth to
the sixteenth centuries is considered Medieval philosophy. Modern philosophy consists in developments from the mid-sixteenth century through the early
nineteenth. Philosophy since the mid-nineteenth century is considered contemporary. All of these labels are loosely used, and indicative features of
each period are found in all subsequent periods.

5. My description of the range of pacifist views generally follows my
earlier account in *From Warism to Pacifism: A Moral Continuum* (Philadel-
phia: Temple University Press, 1989).

6. See Robert Holmes, "Violence and the Perspective of Morality," Chapter One of Holmes' *On War and Morality* (Princeton: Princeton University
Press, 1989).

7. Mohandas K. Gandhi, in *Nonviolent Resistance*, ed. Bharatan Kuma-
rappa (New York: Schocken, 1951).

8. Mulford Q. Sibley, "Concluding Reflections: The Relevance of Nonviolence in Our Day," in *The Quiet Battle*, ed. Mulford Q. Sibley (Boston:
Beacon, 1963), 363-4.

9. Hannah Arendt, *On Violence* (New York: Harcourt Brace Jovanovich,
1969), 63.

10. See Newton Garver, "What Violence Is," in *The Nation* (June 24, 1968),
revised and reprinted in *Today's Moral Problems*, ed. Richard Wasserstrom
(New York: Macmillan, 1975), 410-23.

11. For a helpful discussion of what she calls "isms of domination," see
Karen Warren, "Toward a Feminist Peace Politics," *Journal for Peace and
Justice Studies*, Vol. 3, No. 1 (1991).

12. Holmes, *On War and Morality,* 51.

13. Walzer, *Just and Unjust Wars,* 51.

14. Ibid., 90.

15. Hannah Arendt, *On Violence*, 40.

16. Ramsey Clark, *The Fire This Time: U.S. War Crimes in the Gulf* (New
York: Thunder's Mouth Press, 1992), 59-64.

17. Nelson Mandela, *Long Walk to Freedom* (New York: Little, Brown,
1994), 506-14.

18. Some readers may be surprised to see Nelson Mandela listed with these
more pacifistic exemplary peacemakers since he is notorious for having challenged the African National Congress nonviolence policy and is credited with
founding the ANC army. I include him for two important reasons: first, pacifism admits of degrees, and Mandela seems to fit toward the pragmatic end
of the spectrum; second, despite immense pressure and temptation, given the
violence of the apartheid-based Republic of South Africa he challenged, Man-

dela did not abandon nonviolence.

19. Arendt, *On Violence*, 63.

20. Ibid.

21. Ibid., 52.

22. Mandela, *Long Walk to Freedom*, 235-8.

23. Sara Ruddick, "Fierce and Human Peace," in *Just War, Nonviolence and Nuclear Deterrence*, eds. Duane L. Cady and Richard Werner (Wakefield, NH: Longwood, 1991), 109.

Reply to Professor Cady

In "Pacifist Perspectives on Humanitarian Intervention," Duane Cady makes a passionate and articulate appeal for extreme caution in using force, even in those cases that might fall under the definition of humanitarian intervention In doing this, Professor Cady, like many pacifists, evinces a kind of "love/hate" relationship with the just-war tradition.

Cady correctly delineates the three main ethical perspectives on war that have emerged in the history of philosophy: realism, just war, and pacifism. What I attempt in the following analysis is to examine the idea of pacifism as it is defined by Cady and to ask if that perspective actually advances our understanding of the nature of war and, more importantly, furthers the cause of peace. I also wish to reemphasize that the kind of situation that calls forth humanitarian intervention poses a serious challenge to the varieties of pacifism.

Pacifism and the Just-War Tradition

Cady begins his analysis by somewhat tendentiously describing or labeling as "warism" the view that the use of force in self-defense against unjust aggression is morally justifiable. Unfortunately, it is this kind of language that often leads people to dismiss pacifism, an outcome that Cady laments at various points in his essay. As I understand it, the just-war tradition does not have as its central tenet an illegitimate inference from war as a part of nature to war as morally acceptable. It is a common misunderstanding of the tradition that attributes to it the necessity actually to justify some war or other; or, perhaps more mildly, that if no wars can be morally undertaken, the doctrine has somehow failed. But it is not the role of just-war thinking to advocate the actual prosecution of some war or to provide an ad hoc justification of some past conflict. Its only concern is to specify conditions under which war may be justly initiated and prosecuted. If, for whatever reason, there turn out to be no such conditions, then the conclusion that no war can be morally undertaken is inescapable. But then, the generation of such conclusions is precisely what the theory is all about.

The just-war tradition is properly to be understood not so much as a substantive moral doctrine as a series of questions that any moral agent must ask himself when faced with the question of defense of the rights of others. That is, the just-war tradition presupposes a theory of human goods, but is not itself such a theory.

The just-war provisions intend the implementation of charity in essentially two ways. First, human beings are free and self-determining and their freedom is ordained to certain goods that permit them to flourish. Hence, men must not be deprived of such goods and so are bearers of rights (entitlements) to the basic human goods. If such rights are to be more than a form of words, men must have the power to protect their access to such goods when these come under attack. The right to self-defense against deprivation of the goods is articulated within the just-war tradition, which permits use of force in specific circumstances. The intention of the just-war tradition is not "warism," but the protection of the innocent from those who would deprive them of the means for genuine human flourishing.

Second, acts of self-defense carried out in accord with just-war criteria are, at the same time, acts of charity directed toward the aggressor. For the aggressor is part of the human community and, insofar as his aggression alienates him from that community, neither he nor I can fully flourish. His aggression is, for him, an act of self-mutilation, whereby he closes himself off from his own good by the disrespect he shows to *my* good. As the aggressor does this, he necessarily betrays the larger human community. For this reason, force directed to the restraint or incapacitation of an aggressor is an act of charity for it seeks his good as well as my own. To put it another way, the aggressor's good is inseparable from my good insofar as genuine human fulfillment can only be found in community. It is in this sense that the pacifist is correct: Peace and concord are meant to be the natural condition of man; and so, a key provision of the just war tradition is that the ultimate aim of war must be peace. St. Augustine characterizes the just use of force as "benevolent severity." This "severity" is necessary due to the fallen condition of humanity. The moral law is written on our hearts and can be known and articulated by reason. Yet, human reason has become clouded and subject to concupiscence—an inordinate attachment to creatures. These disordered impulses, to which all are subject in a greater or lesser degree, are the sources of aggression. The purpose of civil society is to ameliorate this disorder by the coercion of criminals domestically and in the repulsion of aggression against the state.

The moral purpose of combat is the removal of the aggressor from the man when diplomacy and other threats and suasions have failed. Hence, war is (or should be) truly a "last resort." The purpose of force used in self-defense is not intentional killing, but restraint or incapacitation. The pacifist critique usually misses this point, but it can be seen most clearly in the POW convention. If a soldier is incapacitated by wounds or other injuries or if he takes himself out of combat through surrender, then in law and morality, it is impermissible to kill him. This is because in both cases (one voluntary, the other involuntary), the aggression has been removed from the man—he has returned to the state of noncombatant. The moral meaning of the POW convention is that killing is not the intention of just force, paradoxical as that may seem, but stopping aggression and, thereby, protecting the innocent while preventing the would-be aggressor from self-harm.

The notion of just force as an act of charity requiring benevolent severity is, for many critics, a serious defect. As Cady notes: "But for the just-war tradition, the evil of war may be necessary for good to prevail in the end. When war is morally chosen it is so not because it is good but because it is seen to be the least evil of available options. This indicates the just-war tradition to be consequentialist in its ethic."

Cady is presumably referring here to the principle of proportionality. But proportionality is not the same thing as consequentialism. As explained in my chapter, the basic human goods that the rules of war seek to protect are incommensurable. It makes no sense to say that they could be weighed against each other or against instances of the same good. The principle of proportionality simply requires that the level of force used against an aggressor not be greater than the threat to the life and rights of the victims. It is very important to note that proportionality has sometimes been used to attempt a consequentialist argument, but this cannot be done. Rather, proportionality is an assessment of alternative choices to be made in light of the principle of fairness. It is not that the lives of the dead are somehow being weighed against the lives of the saved, but that their deaths are accepted as proportional side effects of the effort to resist aggression.

Just-war tradition presupposes that intention and means are "lined up." As John Finnis puts it: "The standard most usually available, and used, for these assessments is the principle of fairness (The Golden Rule or principle of universalizability). This differentiates the impartial from the biased acceptance of harmful side-effects of military action. So, for instance, when the allied air forces followed a policy of precision bombing when attacking German targets in France, and a policy of blind or other imprecise bombing when attacking German targets in Germany, the incidental harm which they were willing to cause by their bombing to German civilians, but unwilling to cause to French civilians, was not accepted by impartial judgment. Assuming the norms of just war tradition, the allies unfairly accepted the harm their bombing caused to German civilians. It is as unfair, not as 'too much' in some other way, that the incidental harm thus accepted is reasonably said to have violated the requirement to proportionality."[1]

Of course, all of this presupposes acceptance of the principle of double effect. And Cady may not concur with this. However, the rejection of double effect would make it impossible to undertake virtually any worthwhile good. It is difficult to think of any projects aimed at furthering basic human goods that would not involve *some* foreseeable risk to other goods. The moral theory behind all this thus holds agents responsible for direct or deliberate damage to (or destruction of) goods, but permits proportional evil as a side effect. As indicated previously, this is not a consequentialist "weighing" of goods (an impossibility in any event), but a reflection of the requirement to participate in basic human goods in a world in which, inevitably, actions have multiple effects. The goal of the moral life is human flourishing through participation in the basic human goods. This requires that each action be open to all of the goods and that no action treat any of these goods as mere means. As long as choices are so directed, it may be possible to permit some extrinsic damage to these goods as a side effect.

The specific application of the principle of double effect to the just-war tradition requires that the use of force be not only a last resort, but that a grave threat be present in the form of imminent danger to life and rights. The kind of threat of which we speak must pose a danger to the integrity of community. Needless to say, force cannot be used to enforce community, as force is inherently antagonistic to the very meaning of community. Again, the main idea is that the just-war tradition has as its object not war, but peace.

Just-War Criteria

Professor Cady also comments on what he believes are frequent misuses of just-war criteria. He believes that there is a selectivity in the application of these and that they are sometimes used as mere rationalizations for the self-interested acts of states. He notes that while the great powers intervened to drive Iraq out of Kuwait, nothing has been done to oust Israel from territory rightly belonging to Egypt, Jordan, Lebanon, and Syria. Moreover, genocide and ethnic cleansing in Pol Pot's Cambodia and in the former Yugoslavia has continued without significant military response from the great powers.

As a general comment, it is important to say that no one is required to do what cannot be done. There are some situations today where military force cannot be successfully employed for strategic or logistical reasons. More specifically, Cady must surely be aware that the case of Israel is *very* different from that of Kuwait. Since the foundation of the State of Israel (a member of the United Nations), Syria, Jordan, Egypt, and others have publicly pledged themselves to the total destruction of the State of Israel and have frequently implemented that pledge with violence. Kuwait, on the other hand, posed no threat whatever to Iraq.

As for Yugoslavia, at this writing, UN hostages have been taken in response to air attacks on Serbian military targets. So, what will now transpire is not clear. However, military interventions must be not only morally justified, but practically possible. There are very compelling arguments of a purely military sort against intervening in the social-cultural mess that is Bosnia today. Combatants and noncombatants are hopelessly and inextricably intertwined. No one has any idea of the proper *goals* of military intervention in this area. It is highly likely that military intervention would merely exacerbate the situation of disorder and death. Certainly, there is general agreement that effective intervention would have to be massive and certainly involve political restructuring, thus going well beyond what are currently thought to be the parameters of justified intervention. All this is quite unlike Kuwait, where the political and military goals, the terrain, and demographics were optimal for intervention. The situation in Bosnia certainly requires intervention, ethically speaking, but the military requirements are on a World War II scale. At least a half-million troops with air and naval support would be needed for nothing short of the conquest, occupation, and political restructuring of Bosnia and, perhaps, Serbia itself. Such an expedition is hardly likely.

Another important consideration is the gravity of the threat. The cogency of the argument for intervention is obviously enhanced by showing that inaction will create ever-widening patterns of evil. This was crucial in the decision to intervene in Kuwait. Cady implies that our intervention there was to preserve cheap oil. Oil was certainly a factor, but only in the sense that Saddam Hussein sought to use oil to subsidize his nuclear weapons program and, thereby, parlay Iraq into world-power status as a nuclear power in the region. It was to prevent that dangerous eventuality that the United Nations sanctioned intervention.

It would, of course, be foolish to deny that states ever intervene selectively. But abuse does not supersede use. The fact that any moral argument, including pacifism, can be corrupted is not a good reason for abandoning such perspectives. The ever-present possibility of misuse should, however, cause us to be keenly aware of inconsistency.

Types of Pacifism

In delineating the types of pacifism, Prof. Cady rejects the "absolute" variety. But in doing so, one wonders if the appellation "pacifism" does not then become more of a liability than an asset. As has been frequently remarked in the literature on war and ethics, what makes pacifism interesting is not the claim that as war involves killing and destruction, every effort should be made to avoid it, but, rather, the belief that it is morally impermissible to use force to repel unjust aggression. It is this radical moral doctrine, consistently applied, that has historically made pacifism either a mark of sainthood or of extreme moral confusion. The hallmark of pacifism has been this kind of moral simplicity. Yet Cady asserts that

". . . most pacifists concede the justifiability of some degree of violence in principle. But rarely are pacifists sympathetic with violence in fact, and when they are it is toward small-scale, interpersonal uses of protective force rather than mass violence, large scale and aggressive." But this statement describes not so much pacifism as a version of the just-war tradition, for it is in terms of proportionality and discrimination that force is judged to be licit. Cady seems to be saying that most pacifists would permit (require?) the use of force if constrained by these conditions. To call this "pacifism" is surely misleading. *A fortiori*, given the historical association of the term "pacifism" with the absolute rejection of force, this description is actually an impediment to the fuller public acceptance of the views advanced by Cady.

Cady laments the fact that most people think pacifists are only impractical dreamers, but this is surely because that term is associated with views quite different from the ones he so lucidly presents. What's in a name? In this case, almost everything.

In this regard, I would also comment on another curiosity. Throughout his presentation, Cady links the pacifist program with opposition to "racism, sexism, and homophobia." I am unclear as to what the connection is here, but it is certain that by including these matters, pacifism is pushed into a somewhat parochial mode. "Racism" and "sexism" are notoriously difficult to pin down, and those who bandy these terms about typically have a highly specific political agenda centered very much in the culture wars of contemporary America. I wonder if it is prudent for pacifists to get involved in these matters.

I also take passing note of the supposed link between pacifism and "homophobia." This term refers to the irrational fear of homosexuals. Now, if anyone has an irrational fear of homosexuals (or anyone/thing else), he should certainly seek professional counseling. But, in fact, "homophobia" is a code word or label applied by homosexual organizations to anyone who refuses to agree that homosexual acts are either morally good or morally neutral. By this ploy, they seek to silence those with moral objections to homosexual acts. A *sexual* union between two persons of the same sex is impossible; hence, a homosexual act necessarily does *violence* to the individuals performing such acts in the root sense of the violation of the order of nature. And, one might add, it is also an indirect attack on "nature's God." So it is somewhat bizarre to find pacifists, of all people, defending such violence.

Conclusion

Professor Cady comes, in the end, to sanction the use of force in
face of what he calls "moral horrors." Here, he seems very close
to Walzer's definition of humanitarian intervention. But he qualifies this by restricting the use of force to ". . . small-scale, clear,
and present dangers from which we can immediately protect ourselves and others by swift, contained violent action . . ." And
again, violence may be warranted ". . . where a swift, controlled
act of violence seems very likely to set straight the scales of justice immediately."

Alas, if only aggressors would tailor their activities to fit such
clear-cut moral miniatures—rather like the classic high-noon shoot-
out on the main street, beloved of the old westerns. I suspect that
many of those who are newly enthusiastic for humanitarian intervention have some such scenario in the back of their minds. But
where are such cases? Cheerleading for humanitarian intervention
based upon projections of such limited and discrete application of
force have very shallow roots in the kind of contemporary situations that call for intervention. The impulse to protect life and rights
divorced from larger considerations of the political structures wherein these definitions are embedded and from which they spring may
turn out to be the Achilles heel of humanitarian intervention.

The case of Somalia is instructive in this regard. The U.S./UN
mission to Somalia had the initial limited purpose of rescuing many
thousands of people from imminent starvation. Their plight was
caused not by an intrinsic shortage of food or chance factors of
nature or demographics, but to the historical fact that Somalia had
been a pawn in the cold war. Always a poor country, Somalia found
itself with a large political vacuum quickly to be filled by political
brigands vying for power and settling old scores. Starvation of parts
of the civil population was clearly a tool of suppression and revenge. For this reason, U.S. forces realized early on that protection
of life and rights could not be separated from the existing political
arrangements. And so, a policy of "nation building," however mut-
ed, had to be undertaken. This entailed efforts to control the various armed factions as a means to political stability. It was at this
point that the "Mogadishu line" was crossed. This expression was
coined by the UN commander Sir David Rose. It marks the transi-
tion from the humanitarian "peace keeping" to the more active

"peace making." That is, U.S. policy makers saw very quickly that a rescue mission focusing strictly upon feeding the hungry would be, at best, a temporary palliative. Yet, nation building would have required a very different and long-term commitment of time, money, and, most crucially, lives. U.S. public opinion rapidly turned against the whole Somalian adventure. All it took was pictures of a serviceman being dragged through the streets and U.S. forces being pinned down by sniper fire coming from the (apparently) erstwhile beneficiaries of our humanitarian intervention. U.S. forces pulled out amid scenes reminiscent of Saigon two decades earlier. Somalia is now back to square one and, we may assume, it is only a matter of time until life and rights are again at risk.

There is hardly likely to be much enthusiasm for a similar expedition. While one understands and supports Cady's desire for restricted interventions, if they are on the model of current efforts, the prognosis is not good.

Perhaps a more hopeful example is Haiti. At this writing, it appears that U.S. intervention there has been a success and that such a happy outcome as has been achieved is directly connected with the political dimension of the matter. Use of force in Haiti was in aid of restoring a duly elected President Jean-Bertrand Aristide to his rightful office. The fact that political reform or restoration, rather than direct humanitarian intervention, was central and defining in the U.S. mission perhaps accounts for the relative success of that undertaking (thus far). This might provide a criterion for intervention if the Haiti case did not seem to be such a rarity among situations requiring intervention.

The great revolution in contemporary thinking has recognized that borders are not inviolable in face of human suffering and oppression. Increasingly, the world understands the moral unity of the human race. This is the great virtue of the ideology behind humanitarian intervention. It gives force in international law and in the practice of nations to the moral ideals of justice and love of neighbor. It would be a great loss to squander this moral capital. That could happen if we have another Somalia.

The next step in the development of the practice of humanitarian intervention will be the most difficult. If we are not to lose the moral and psychological advantage gained by the shift toward theories of humanitarian intervention, it will be necessary to clearly

articulate the connection between the agreed-upon humanitarian
categories of life and rights and the political/social/cultural structures necessary to support them. As I have noted, we need to avoid
the Hobbesian trap of thinking that moral duty is satisfied through
the abstract imperative to save life. The very same insight that led
away from the inviolability of sovereignty (that peace is not the sole
good) should lead us to a more robust conception of humanitarian
intervention as requiring a structural setting that will guarantee the
long-term preservation of life and rights.

There is certainly a danger that popular support for humanitarian intervention so understood might diminish. For it is obvious that
the kind of military/political commitment necessary to sustain long-
term rights will be significantly greater than the "hit-and-run" strategy that appears to underpin current theories of humanitarian
intervention. However, there is really no alternative if we want to
avoid the Somalia syndrome. What we have now is an effort to
assuage moral conscience on the cheap.

What all this means is that supranational organizations, regional
alliances, and, most of all, the UN will become key players. Minimally, this would indicate a revived UN command capable of long-
term commitment. This was something envisaged in the original
Charter as a more or less permanent UN military force with its own
chain of command. The tensions of the Cold War made such an
arrangement impossible, but current conditions suggest a revival of
the idea. Military force so conceived would need to be backed by
the ample diplomatic, technical, and political expertise of the various UN agencies. Such assets are, after all, currently available. The
problem is political will, which especially concerns the United States.

There is a strong current of neo-isolation in the political blood-
stream at this moment. While the majority of voters appear to support a bipartisan internationalist approach, those who would revive
an "America First" stance are extremely vocal and can be expected
to influence foreign policy by making leadership much more cautious regarding military interventions. While George Bush's popu-
larity soared to an all-time record high in the wake of the successful
intervention in the Gulf War, it did him little political good in the
election. This lesson was not lost on Bill Clinton, who talked tough
over Bosnia during the presidential campaign, but quickly reversed
course on taking office. The recent interventions and proposed interventions presented to the American public have left most people

cold. Most Americans do not understand the point of these interventions and when even the most minimal casualties result, the cry
for withdrawal is heard throughout the land. While the average
American will confess to the need to help others and will understand the connection between American security and a peaceful
world, unless the rationale of *specific* interventions is clearly spelled
out, he will be a very reluctant supporter.

The growth of neo-isolationism is in direct proportion to this inability of political leadership to inspire confidence in the moral
and political rectitude of current foreign policy initiatives with a
military component. And unless politicians can perceive some political assets in these foreign adventures, they are likely to support
them with words, rather than actions. The reason why this is critical is that only the United States possesses the capability for global
military projection. In a recent comment, President Clinton chas-
tised the neo-isolationists for their nonsupport of the United Nations by noting that if the UN failed, the United States would have
to carry the ball in maintaining global peace. What the president
appears not to understand is that even if the UN works perfectly,
America will still have to bear the primary burden. This is because
it is not realistic to expect countries such as Britain and France to
mount the type of defense outlay that provides the United States
with a multipronged defense capability. Moreover, it is no secret
that it is not really in the interest of America that some other power or group of powers should build a defense establishment to rival
that of the United States. This is not to say that other countries are
powerless, but that any sustained intervention will have to have U.S.
support. Thus, the claim (made by both liberals and conservatives)
that America cannot be "the policeman of the world" runs up against
the stubborn fact that there is no one else to assume the role.

In conclusion, I fully agree with Cady's comment: "The challenge is creating and sustaining conditions where life may flourish,
where order is internalized, cooperative and respectful of human
rights rather than conditions of misery where order is imposed,
exploitive, domineering and abusive. [And, again,] Our struggle is
to foster conditions that preclude or at least reduce powerlessness,
that encourage participation, cooperation and internal sustaining
order."

But such outcomes cannot be obtained by isolating a category
of "humanitarian goods" and seeking to protect these while

ignoring the social and political context. The long-overdue recognition in ethics and international law that persons are bearers of rights, which transcend national borders and political regimes, must always be understood as conditioned by the inevitability of political community. Professor Cady's "sustaining conditions where life may flourish" are inseparable from the right to life itself.

Note

1. John Finnis, Joseph Boyle, and German Grisez, *Nuclear Deterrence, Morality, and Realism* (Oxford: Oxford University Press, 1987), 253.

Reply to Professor Phillips

In "The Ethics of Humanitarian Intervention," Robert Phillips has provided an articulate explanation and defense of traditional just-warism. He locates his discussion within the contemporary post-cold war world and offers an account of shifting dominant values on what he calls the doctrine of nonintervention—the inclination of nations to respect one another's borders—by tracing the history of the nation-state in Western European culture. Phillips anchors his own ethical perspective squarely in established Judeo-Christian thought, defending a natural-law notion of universal ethics and giving us his own blend of communitarian and Catholic perspectives. He sees intervention to have an important place in upholding justice in a world community and justifies military force as an extension of charity.

In what follows I will explicate and critique several of Phillips's arguments and explore their implications from a pacifist perspective. Following a broad review of Phillips's position, my critical focus will be on what I take to be the main points of contention between his defense of just-warism and the range of pacifist views: 1) the presumption that violent intervention can secure justice despite the historical record, 2) the tension/dilemma/contradiction of employing violent means in search of peaceful ends, and 3) the suggestion that governments must choose between suffering acceptance (passivism) and violence to defend justice, i.e., the virtual absence of consideration for nonviolent actions in defense of justice.

One further comment is in order before going on with this response. It should be clear to those having read both lead essays in this volume that just-warist and pacifist perspectives on humanitarian intervention are not simple and clear polar opposites; rather, they consist of a wide variety of positions that differ more in degree than in kind. The version of just-warism defended by Professor Phillips requires considerably more moral restraint on military force than do popular views of the dominant culture. Yet at the same time it requires significantly less moral restraint on violence than do the varieties of pacifism described above. This means that the differences between Phillips's restrained just-warism and weaker forms of pacifism will be much closer than some readers may have anticipated. This "softening" of just-warism is movement in the right direction; violence would be much reduced were more just-warists to share Phillips's restrained view and were governments actually to act within such restraints. Yet pacifists press for even more movement along the value continuum, still further away from arguments designed to permit violence and ever closer to recognizing that positive peace, the goal shared by just-warists and pacifists alike, can only be built nonviolently.

Overview

Phillips opens his defense of military intervention by noting that the post-World War II Cold War had provided a structure for international conflict wherein the United States and the Soviet Union each acted in efforts to contain the other. He notes that this structure may have restrained superpowers from full-scale war while acknowledging that many nations suffered as Cold War pawns. The Vietnam War provoked increasing reluctance to engage militarily; more and more the role of the military has been to deter other military activity. With the collapse of the Soviet Union, the strategy of containment gave way to a new world disorder without effective supranational systems to manage increasing nationalism, political fragmentation and human rights violations in need of policing. Wary of self-serving governmental rhetoric, Phillips suggests that analysis of interventions focus not only on intentions but also on means and outcomes.

Before constructing his defense of intervention in our contemporary world disorder, Phillips sketches a history of state sovereignty, paying particular attention to the notion of state autonomy. He argues that the Enlightenment, and with it the idea of reason as primary and universal, gave rise to an internationalism of human uniformity that was in tension with the particularity of peoples, nations, ethnicities, and religions. This led to efforts to eradicate the "irrationality of particularity" by force. For Phillips, human completeness is only achieved in cultures; community provides context for human good. This explains the strong presumption against any intervention, since intervention would violate the particularity of cultures. At the same time Phillips defends a universal human nature, and with it universal human good. Culture is important, yet not absolute. But his notion of human good stems not from Enlightenment reason; rather, it is based within traditional Christian natural moral law. Phillips sees military intervention to be an exception to the warranted presumption of nonintervention, an exception required by universal justice. As such, intervention by military force is a matter of charity, not just morally permitted and but sometimes morally required, of "helping people to help themselves."

Bereft of religion, ethnicity, and historical particularity, Enlightenment reason imposes uniformity and reflects, for Phillips, the *Realpolitik* principles and practices of Hobbes, Machiavelli, and the modern nation-state. Under a Western ideological hegemony, sovereignty has been transformed from a relative status, guaranteed by Christian princes under natural law, to an absolute status conceived in realism and increasingly written into international law. Himself anchored in Christian natural law, Phillips tries to preserve particularity while using universal morality to justify military intervention in service to humanitarian justice. He appeals to guidelines and restraints from the just-war tradition to check possible abuses of his moral argument for intervention, and includes a review of Walzer's defense of intervention and commentary on a recent report of the Wilton Park Conference on the United Nations in the New World Disorder to round out his position. The result is a cautious and restrained just-warist perspective that sees military intervention to be the least objectionable option available to charitable nations in service to justice.

Having sketched an overview of Phillips's just-war perspective on military intervention, I will follow his suggestion that analysis of such views must consider not only intention but also means and outcomes. Particular pacifists would contest many differing points with Professor Phillips; I must speak broadly about the range of pacifist response.

I can understand Phillips's reluctance to embrace a thoroughgoing moral relativism, which, as he says, sacrifices justice to an absolute doctrine of nonintervention. And I can understand his

reluctance to endorse imposing a uniform brand of justice as absolute for everyone, everywhere, for all time; as he says, such dog-
matism would ignore important cultural and historic particularities.
This leaves him struggling to find a middle ground neither too restrictive nor too permissive when it comes to using violence in the
cause of justice. Various just-warists and pacifists across the value
continuum on morality and violence share this dilemma despite major
differences over the grounds of their morality. Phillips and I both
contend with this dilemma since neither of us is absolutist in our
view. Our differences are matters of degree. My defense of the
pacifist perspective at this juncture is grounded in the three points
of contention I mentioned briefly at the outset of this response. I
will now turn to a development of each of them.

The History of Violent Intervention

Professor Phillips insists that any analysis of intervention must focus on intentions, means, and outcomes. He is (understandably) wary
of intentions; much of the public policy debate turns almost exclusively on intentions and this aspect of intervention is most easily
distorted by national self-interest, political ideology, and even the
crass and personal self-interests of those in positions to influence
policy. Interventions tend to be undertaken by major powers, which
have security as well as political and economic interests to protect.
The military portion of major-power economies is substantial, and
a great deal of corporate and personal wealth is connected with
weapons policies and activities. Articulate proponents of virtually
any intervention can and do appropriate the language of the moral
tradition, demonize the enemy, cloak prudential national or other
interests in moral terms, and thereby "justify" military action. Phillips's own defense of military intervention as an extension of
charity is itself vulnerable because determining whether a given
act qualifies as charity is in large part dependent on intention.
While debate over intentions is important to test and expose misap-
propriations of morality, Phillips must insist on analysis of means
and outcomes; the proof is in the pudding, not the self-described
recipe.

Turning to means, it is interesting to note that the just war tradition generally and Phillips's defense in particular focus exclusively
on violent, military force as the means of humanitarian intervention. It is simply taken for granted that state violence is a nation's

way of doing international business. Phillips's entire effort of exploring humanitarian intervention is dedicated to justifying permission for the use of violent, military force. Alternative means are treated as if they are nonexistent; worse, they are defined out of existence by their omission. The presumption is that nations either do nothing, ignoring and allowing the human rights abuses calling for attention, or nations take up arms and send in troops. Presuming there are no other options is tantamount to being without other options. More will be said about alternative means of intervention below. For now, the focus must be on testing violent military means against their outcomes.

If the proof is to be in the pudding, all we can do is look at history and judge the success of military means to secure justice by violent intervention. Needless to say, anything even approaching an exhaustive consideration of, say, post-World War II major power interventions is well beyond the scope of this response. The task is simply too great, given the propensity of nations to intervene, allegedly on humanitarian grounds. In this space, we can only look broadly, and at just a few important cases, to try to form judgments on the efficacy of military intervention. Despite the inevitable limitations of any selection of cases, there is little doubt as to pacifist perspectives on the issue.

A number of cases leap to mind as we begin to reflect on important interventions of the past few decades; Vietnam, Afghanistan, Lebanon, Iraq, Somalia, Chechnya, and Haiti are just a few. And how does weighing outcomes against means inform us about the relative wisdom of intervention? Did the outcome of the war in Vietnam outweigh the evils of the deaths, injuries, destruction, dislocation and other consequences of the violent means employed by participants, including the contributions the war made to subsequent events in the region, like Pol Pot's reign of terror? How was justice served by the years of war? Was this international charity? By most accounts, the US intervention in Vietnam has been considered a tragic mistake.

Or, to take another case, consider the consequences of the Gulf War, certainly devastating for ordinary Iraqis as well as for the army of Iraq. Certainly US military morale was boosted by so quick and easy a victory, and a renegade regional power which threatened to inhibit the flow of oil fueling Western economies was put down, at least for a time. Yet when the full outcome is weighed, was justice served by such thorough destruction, so many civilian as well as military deaths, such total annihilation of the infrastructure of Iraq? And what has changed in the way of establishing a just and peaceful order both within Iraq and among Iraq and neighboring nations?

Beyond Vietnam and Iraq, can we honestly say the "outcomes" test would go any better for the cases of Afghanistan, Lebanon, Somalia, Chechnya, or a host of other cases we might take up? It seems not. In each case the intentions and expectations widely missed the outcomes.

Haiti seems different. While the long-term implications of the US occupation are unclear at this writing, the situation does seem markedly improved at least in the short term, with US and UN troops in place to provide stability, policing, training, and support for the Aristide government. For pacifists, the intervention in Haiti is much harder to condemn than the others cited; for just-warists, it's much easier to defend. When we compare this situation with the others, the contrasts are glaring. In Haiti the elected government invited the occupying forces, the intervention was on a small scale, high-level negotiations preceded the action, and the intervention itself has involved very little violence from the occupying troops. Their work seems more akin to police work than military invasion. Still, the Haiti case is not a clear and easy one for pacifists to condone; certainly motives for intervention were at best mixed, with U.S. governmental and private citizen interests at stake, given the long and often bitter history of economic and political exploitation of Haitians by Americans.

Clearly, the historical study of intervention is a vast and difficult undertaking; here we have given only very brief consideration and to just a few cases. They are meant more to illustrate pacifist perspectives and to suggest taking a critical attitude toward adventurist and interventionist foreign policy than to provide definitive proof of anything. But when we reflect on outcomes, history seems to suggest a greater likelihood of satisfying the goal to serve justice if interventions are small-scale, limited, and controlled police-like actions supervised internationally. And we reduce the likelihood of serving justice when interventions are large-scale, open-ended military actions of single nations.

This leaves us with pacifists and just-warists less at odds than conventional wisdom suggests. While pacifists toward the absolutist end of the spectrum condemn all violent interventions, many pacifists are not absolutists and condone varying degrees of force in service to justice. This does not, however, make pacifism and just-warism collapse into one another. Pacifist opposition to large-scale violence precludes supporting war; just-warists can justify violence on a larger scale than can pacifists and thus can justify war. Admittedly, it is not easy to draw a line between large-scale police work and small-scale war. Pacifists may disagree with one another as well as with warists about making such a distinction; so too for warists. But difficulty in drawing a fine line in murky cases does not mean there are no clear cases. The point is that pacifists oppose war on moral grounds. Alleged "policing" actions that take on the scale of war cannot be excused. Even if all war is wrong, still, some wars can be more or less wrong than others. Scale is an important factor.

Those holding views along the pacifist continuum are eager to subject interventions to the outcomes test. Pacifists may disagree with one another over details and fine points of various cases yet they unite generally in challenging just-warists to cite cases from history where outcomes warrant the violent means, where justice was clearly served. For pacifists, the lessons of history reveal carnage, suffering, and destruction; corpses, amputees, and refugees; bitterness, loss and emptiness; often resulting from righteous moral justifications and noble causes not fixed, indeed not fixable by violence. "Successful" interventions are so rare that they should be considered exceptions rather than be used to inspire and justify future intervention.

Means and Ends

A second point of contention between Phillips's just-war interventionism and the range of pacifist perspectives is the inevitable dilemma/tension/contradiction inherent in any just-warist position: the means of military intervention are at odds with the ends sought. More than this, means and ends are not merely at odds, they are incompatible, contradictory. By what logic can one claim to create peace through violence?

The separation of means and ends is a necessary part of any just-war position because warists readily admit that the means of war are awful. War is not good in itself; those who think military violence is justifiable construct their justifications by appealing to the ends as sufficiently good to outweigh the evil means. Or they claim that without violent means even worse outcomes will result. Either

way the violence of the means is claimed to be offset by the results, and the outcome is the crux of the matter. The just-war case
against pacifism is that pacifism is so tied to nonviolent means that
it allows injustice to triumph.

Meanwhile, pacifists wonder how violence begets peace. Seeing
outcomes as natural extensions of the means to them, pacifists wonder how one could build trust by dishonest means, create cooperation by coercive means, or achieve respect by threatening means.
For pacifists, means and ends cannot be so contradictory, nor can
they be so neatly separated. Results achieved from any action flow
inevitably from the means undertaken. Peace is not an isolated objective—an outcome—but a way of living and interacting. As the
acorn is to the oak tree, so are means related to ends. We reap what
we sow. The means and ends of peace coalesce.

Consider for a moment the polar extremes in this debate: acting
on principle *regardless* of consequences on the one hand (an absolute pacifist might serve as an example here), and acting for the
sake of certain results *regardless* of what means we might use on
the other (a hard-line warist is an example here). When we compare these polar-opposite considerations to what ordinary individuals do when attempting to lead a moral life, we recognize at once
the artificiality of either of these extreme ways of conceiving moral deliberations. Most of us, most of the time, weigh various outcomes and various means along with a host of other considerations
in coming to ethical decisions. Often, when we think of being moral we think of being kind, honest, and generous; caring for family
and friends; having compassion for those in need; maintaining integrity; avoiding cruelty; not lying or stealing; and so on. And if
we think of means and ends at all, we seek means that are compatible with ends. Our moral objectives are not separate from our decisions and activities; they are extensions of them. So the polar
opposition, the dichotomy of this debate, is unreal to our experience.

The upshot for pacifists is that being moral is not manipulating
means to force ends; a moral life is an integrated one where our
attitudes, decisions, and activities are harmonious with our goals.
All of this is reminiscent of the brief discussion of virtue ethics
above.[1] On a virtue-ethics model, morality is not a simple matter
of doing one's duty or generating certain outcomes. Rather, the good
life is a matter of character, of fulfillment, of excellence in certain
virtues, like self-control or peacefulness. I raise this here not to force

a choice among deontological, teleological and virtue ethics, but to call attention to the subtlety and complexity of morality and to broaden our consideration of it. Different sorts of warists and pacifists accept or reject various interventions for a diverse and complicated array of reasons. Recognizing this complexity challenges the "outcomes" test by insisting that other factors, like compatibility of means to ends as well as one's sense of integrity, are relevant considerations.

Pacifists often challenge the neat separation of means and ends. In doing so, they undercut the just-warist strategy of excusing or condoning violent means on the hope of achieving results good enough to outweigh the evils of those means. It is not that pacifists neglect outcomes; rather, they see moral choice and action as involving much more than results. In fact, good results can be spoiled by the means employed to gain them. Even if wealth is a good, gaining it by theft is not moral. This brings us to the third major point of contention between pacifists and just-warists on violent intervention, i.e., nonviolent actions in defense of justice.

Nonviolent Intervention

Warism is a prevailing outlook in our world. Violence is simply taken for granted as a perfectly normal, natural, and moral response to injustice. In fact, warism is so prevalent that it is a given; something is thought to be wrong with anyone who even entertains thoughts of nonviolent direct action in the face of injustice. Warism is the context in which intervention is discussed. One result is that the burden of proof is on nonviolence; violence is the norm, the accepted and even required means to advance justice.

We have briefly examined pacifist challenges to the presumption of violence in two ways above, questioning the widely held belief that violent intervention in fact yields good outcomes, and challenging the logic of using means incompatible with desired ends. Now we must examine the warist inclination to treat nonviolent means for creating and defending justice as if they don't exist. In the process of this examination I will argue not only that they exist and are available for use, but further that *only* nonviolent means can build the positive peace needed to sustain justice.

A major obstacle in recognizing nonviolence is the prevailing concept of peace. Peace is widely taken to be the absence of violence, the absence of war. I have called this notion "negative peace" above because it carries no positive characteristics. For those who understand peace in this way, we know it when we see it because it is not violent and it is not warlike. The challenge to pacifists is to help those holding prevailing warist beliefs to see nonviolence, to see positive peace, and to recognize the emptiness of negative peace. As long as our best idea of peace is the absence of violence, peace is not real for us and we will continue to choose violence as a means to our goals.

There is a great deal more to genuine peace than the mere absence of violence. Genuine or positive peace is the presence of social, national, and international order arising from among participants by cooperation, not merely order imposed from outside by force. But if positive peace exists, why is it so easy to overlook? The truth is, positive peace is so much a part of our daily routine that we fail to realize that we are making and sustaining it with every cooperative act. When people participate meaningfully in organizing their lives and constructing social policy; when police use force only in noninjurious, discriminating, and restrained ways; when courts adjudicate public law fairly; when conflict is resolved nonviolently; when gross imbalances of economic, personal, social, or national power are kept in check; then genuine positive peace is present. Clearly, all of this happens to varying degrees in different contexts much of the time. The point is that peace is not simply the absence of violence; it is the presence of a great deal else. It goes unnoticed because violations of such conditions command our attention when they intrude, so much so that we take peace to be the absence of such violations.

Cooperative and collaborative acts often seem natural among individuals with shared interests, history, and values. But individuals with much in common can be fierce competitors as well. Likewise, diverse collections of people, those with differing interests, histories, and values may be expected to be at odds socially, politically, and economically. But they need not be so; cooperative and collaborative behavior may characterize those with little in common beyond the will to build peace. While peace arises from within groups, it can be broken from the outside by exploitation, oppression, violence, and other forms of violation. Since the breaking is so intrusive and disturbing, we focus on breaches of the peace and think of peace as the absence of violence. And since genuine peace arises from within groups, groups tend to be wary of other groups, especially if there are no members common to both groups.

Once we begin to understand peace as a positive presence—involving participation, choice, cooperation, respect, mutuality, and community—we begin to realize that violent force cannot create it. As Spinoza put it, in his *Theological-Political Treatise*, "Peace is not an absence of war, it is a virtue, a state of mind, a disposition for benevolence, confidence, justice." Coercion, violent force, threats and intimidation do not incline us to cooperative, participatory community, except, perhaps, to cooperate in mounting retaliatory coercion, violence, or threats. Even if such responses weld communities together in their hostility toward another group, they do not precipitate genuine peace among the contending groups; only nonviolence can do that.

Clearly, taking up violence can satisfy the desire to "do something" to counter violence, invasion, and injustice. It can satisfy an urge for revenge, and occasionally it can set a temporary negative peace in place, at least for the term of an occupation. But negative peace wrought through violence is at best a begrudging concession of a beaten, resentful, and humiliated enemy. Pretended cooperation lasts only as long as the coercion holding it in place. The events of the past decade in Eastern Europe offer ample reminders of the lasting value of inauthentic peace.

Genuine peace involves willful participation, cooperative and collaborative activities, and a sense of community. These are created not by violence or threat of violence but by care, trust, respect, and equality; that is, by mutuality. Whereas genuine peace is complex, fragile, and develops slowly, violence can erupt quickly out of an insistent and dogmatic urge for immediate change. Destruction is quick; creation is slow. Powerlessness, frustration, impatience, and injustice all tempt us to seize the means of violence to achieve the ever elusive quick fix. This is why violence continues to be a problem. Violence is quick and easy; peace, genuine peace, is slow and hard.

People of good will with deep concerns for justice continue to choose violence in part out of habit, in part out of despair. Weary of outrages against justice, conditioned to traditional violent means, hopeful of saving victims from cruelty or slaughter, they take up tools of destruction to destroy destroyers, hoping for a quick shortcut to the genuine peace they desire. By offering moral justifications for their violence they confirm and sustain the dominant notion that violence can be moral, and they reinforce their enemies' moral resolve. The pattern continues in self-reinforcing cycles.

This point of contention between pacifist and just-warist perspectives concerning nonviolence is crucial. Pacifists contend not only that nonviolence is preferable to violence in creating and sustaining genuine peace, but also that nonviolence is essential for the task and that violence is incapable of it. Thus, if intervention is in order, if it is to be humanitarian, and if it is to have lasting, genuine outcomes, it should be nonviolent.

Since I have sketched nonviolent means of intervention above, they need not be repeated here. The point is that there are nonviolent means to further justice, in fact only nonviolent means further genuine peace, so the common just-warist suggestion that if we are not to intervene violently then we must be passive and acquiesce to evil is simply false. We have a host of options, all of the means of justice used in the cooperative, collaborative, community-sustaining aspects of life. The greater the support for and cooperation with nonviolent intervention actions both internationally and within the nation in need of intervention, the greater the likelihood of genuine peace being created and sustained. As Hannah Arendt puts it, "the extreme form of power is All against One; the extreme form of violence is One against All."[2] Just as violence begets more violence, nonviolence begets cooperative, collaborative, internal order based on mutuality. Attempts to impose order from the outside by force do not create internal order; rather, they create resentment and resistance.

Space limitations preclude a review of specific nonviolent, direct humanitarian interventions here, but obvious cases can be recalled. Perhaps the most remarkable and encouraging example in recent years is the nonviolent transformation of the Republic of South Africa. Although it took years, the international cooperative pressure on South Africa, including divestment in corporations doing business there, excluding South African participation in international sporting events, artists from many nations refusing to perform there, and so on, all contributed mightily to minimizing violence in the democratization of the nation. Complex and difficult as the process was, who would suggest that violent intervention might have been better?

There are no guarantees that nonviolence will always work; but we need to remember that violence rarely works to bring peace, and when it does it is temporary and negative peace. Threats and acts of violence cannot create and sustain genuine internal order. Sadly, the warist predispositions of the dominant culture provide a climate in which violence is cherished as courageous and decisive while nonviolence is widely considered cowardly and weak. The burden of proof is put on nonviolence to earn credibility while violence is taken for granted as effective and moral. This is conventional wisdom; critical reflection exposes such presumptions to be mistaken.

The prevailing warist modes of operation have been cloaked in moral justifications and have created an overarmed, belligerent, dangerous, and hostile set of contentious nation-states. The war system has repeatedly failed to produce lasting genuine peace. Recent public reflections on options in Bosnia, for example, reveal that even military leaders are acknowledging the limits, even the obsolescence, of the war system. Even the military is reluctant to get involved in war because they have little confidence that peace can be won. Once the shortcomings and likely failure of violent means to peace become apparent, only then are advocates of nonviolence consulted and asked for suggestions. And at that point pacifists are expected to produce an immediate nonviolent fix despite generations of dedicated warist work to the contrary. When they cannot, because genuine peace is complex, difficult and slow, and the problems in need of fixing are deep, longstanding and have been exacerbated by generations of violence and warism, then nonviolence is dismissed as naive and ineffectual. And why is it that war is not so easily dismissed on the basis of its history of failure? Might it be that war has been and is primarily an instrument of acquisition, elevation, imposition, and violation, hardly an instrument of charity?

Conclusion

Humanitarian intervention is, indeed, a complex and difficult issue. Considering the range of moral views across war-realist, just-war, and pacifist perspectives should disabuse us of the urge to hold simplistic positions. Differences between just-war and pacifist

perspectives turn out to be matters of degree, not the polar opposi-
tions of conventional wisdom.

Despite softening the opposition between just-warists and pacifists on intervention, the perspective I have described here remains
well within the pacifist range of views. While pacifists can and do
disagree about the bases and extent of their pacifism, both in theory and in application to particular cases, there is broad pacifist con-
vergence over moral opposition to violence and war as well as broad
moral disposition toward social and political order that arises from
within groups as distinct from order imposed onto groups from the
outside.

In this response to Professor Phillips's defense of traditional just-
war intervention, I have tried to highlight what I take to be the three
primary points of contention between just-warists and pacifists of
various sorts. Pacifists challenge the warist presumption that violent intervention can secure just peace by suggesting that a review
of the historical record suggests otherwise. Second, pacifists challenge the logic of violent intervention by underscoring the tension,
dilemma, and contradiction of attempting to secure lasting, genuinely peaceful ends by using violently coercive means. Finally, pacifists challenge the virtual lack of consideration given by just-warists
to nonviolent means to create and sustain peaceful social and political order. The point is not merely to indicate an oversight, or even
to suggest omitted alternatives to violent intervention. Rather, the
point is to understand that *only* nonviolence can generate the internal order characteristic of genuine peace, so violence must always
fail in the long run.

Humans have labored too long under the burdens of war and
violence. The burdens are many, and they are heavy. Not only do
humans bear death, destruction, dislocation, and suffering as victims, but also moral burdens, burdens of conscience, as victimiz-
ers, as perpetrators of violence. Economic, social, psychological, and
political burdens must be born. And all of these burdens are passed
along from generation to generation.

As I have said, violence and destruction are quick and easy;
peace and creation are slow and difficult. Varieties of pacifism do
not pretend to offer quick and immediate solutions to the many
problems prompting violence in our world. But they do allow us to
step back from the escalating horrors that choosing violence
has given us. The range of pacifist thought challenges us to do bet-

ter than follow the dominant predispositions to warism. Pacifism challenges us to think carefully and critically and to get
beyond violence, a failed means of social order, to imagine and create the nonviolent world all of us seek. The first step is thinking it
possible.

Notes

1. Cf. p. 39–40.
2. Hannah Arendt, *On Violence* (New York: Harcourt Brace Jovanovich,
1969), 42.

Index

About the Authors

Robert L. Phillips is professor of philosophy and director of the War and Ethics Program at the University of Connecticut. He is the author of *War and Justice* (University of Oklahoma Press, 1984) as well as numerous articles and book chapters. Professor Phillips is on the editorial boards of several journals and is a frequent commentator on radio and television concerning issues of international violence.

Duane L. Cady is professor of philosophy and department chair at Hamline University. He is the author of *From Warism to Pacifism: A Moral Continuum* (Temple University Press, 1989), co-editor (with Richard Werner) of *Just War, Nonviolence and Nuclear Deterrence* (Longwood, 1991), and co-editor (with Karen Warren) of *Bringing Peace Home: Feminism, Violence and Nature* (Indiana University Press, forthcoming). Professor Cady's essays on ethics and history of philosophy have appeared in various journals including *Philosophical Studies, Philosophy and Social Criticism, Hypatia*, and *The Journal of Social Philosophy*. He is a past president of Concerned Philosophers for Peace.